DISTRACTED AND DEFEATED

the rulers and the ruled

by
MIKE BHANGU

bbp

ISBN 978-0-9940799-4-7 (paperback) — ISBN 978-0-9940799-3-0 (epub)

Library and Archives Canada Cataloguing in Publication

Bhangu, Mike Singh, author
    Distracted and defeated : the rulers and the ruled / Mike Bhangu.

Issued in print and electronic formats.
ISBN 978-0-9940799-4-7 (paperback).—ISBN 978-0-9940799-3-0 (epub)

    1. Social change. 2. Social classes. 3. Popular culture—Political aspects. I. Title.

HM831.B43 2017   **303.4**   **C2015-905078-2**
                                             C2015-905079-0

Illustrator: Mike Bhangu
Published by BB Productions
British Columbia, Canada
thinkingmanmike@gmail.com

I DEDICATE THIS BOOK TO THE SHEEP WHO ROAR LIKE LIONS.

I SALUTE YOU.

Table of Contents

Preface

Introduction

Chapter 1: Ante Bellum

Disagreement over the Social Contract

Near Defeat

The Old is New

Decoding Life

Bread and Circuses

Dead Heroes and Gangsters

To Believe

Artificial Inflation

The Big O

Pleasure-Seekers

Abstinence

Love as a Distraction

Soulmate

The Art of Mating

Liquor, Nicotine, and Things

Alcohol and Disunity

Individuality

A False Notion of Success

Sheep Make Sheep

Gears and Grease

The Chase

How They Do It

Master and Servant

To Want

To Repeat

Provocateur

To Submit

Table of Contents

Table of Contents

Preface

From time to time, the "haves" of society shape and manipulate the type of information the "have-nots" absorb and become.

The "haves" tamper with information so to control the type of thoughts and actions the "have-nots" might conjure. If the "have-nots" were free to think freely, they might challenge the status quo. If the current state of affairs is modified, "the haves" might lose their status as "the haves" and the power they're accustomed to.

The accumulation of each instance has birthed an illusion and every person is subject to the misinformation. To make matters worse, most people are born with a trusting mindset and do not expect the deception. Nor are they prepared for it.

The mystery is worldwide and evident throughout written history. The manner in which the world is presented isn't complete and fabrications are scattered throughout the chronology.

....

Whatever it may be, the dye was cast and I be who I be. Built to challenge, built to be broken, and built to be rebuilt. Welcome to my world.

Introduction

The power to bring about positive social change hibernates. If it doesn't soon wake, I'm afraid a coma it might taste.

A deep sleep might be the consequence and the beneficiaries of unity are those who stand dazed and separate. From their respective islands, each abandons their only real strength—unity.

Nevertheless, I know better than to blame the person. Now and again, the information our popular culture communicates, the information people use to construct values, tactfully misdirects an individual from realizing their designation.

This isn't a new age happening. The regulators understand how to influence the thoughts of an individual and they've employed this stratagem from the very beginning of society. It's an effective method of maintaining their power.

Strategies exercised far before the Roman Emperors and the Egyptian Pharaohs. Tactics still exploited by the contemporary elite of the world. Sometimes, it feels as if nothing much has changed but names and titles.

I know, I know. You're an individual and above manipulation. Unfortunately, what the human creature is isn't. An individual thinks and behaves in accordance to their value system—a person will define their reality in agreement with the information contained within. It's the nature of the human. The individual is designed this way. Tragically, this predisposition is easily exploited.

Those who rule, from time to time, stage-manage ideas, information, and knowledge. They do that to maintain and enhance the status quo. In this reality, the individual is unendingly misdirected by beliefs, wants, and expectations while the rulers remain the overlords. Moreover, under this artificial dome of knowledge, most people fail to comprehend the sub-human and synthetic continuum they're trapped into.

Instead of lifting the people's awareness and showing them a better individual and a better world, the masters of the machine, from time to time, feed the public a value system that doesn't enhance the human experience. Categorized under five chapters, this manuscript identifies some of the tactics, artificial circumstances, and values that distract the people from realizing the exploitative situation they were born to, and from uniting under one banner and improving their living standard.

Chapter 1: Ante Bellum
Only in unity can the people bring forth better conditions so to improve each individual's existence. Only in unity can one reach their fullest potential. But distracted, and inevitably divided, all efforts are easily thwarted. This chapter introduces several of the beliefs that distract the people from higher intentions and realizing their underdeveloped disposition.

Chapter 2: Chameleon
This chapter will explore popular media's contribution to the theme of this manuscript.

Chapter 3: Gubernatio
"The power is in the people and politics we address." — Tupac Shakur

Chapter 4: Self-Sabotage

The greatest obstacles hindering the becoming of a better world and a higher living standard are those who will benefit. The greatest enemies are the enemies within. More specifically, the wants, beliefs, and expectations that create conflict and prevent a united front.

Chapter 5: The Last Hope

The last line of defence is openly assaulted and so many silently sit in the audience. This chapter will examine how the family unit is under attack.

CHAPTER 1
ANTE BELLUM

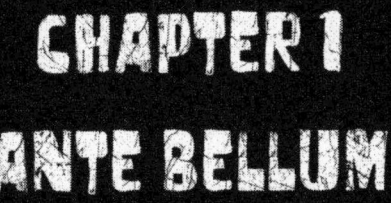

Only in unity can the people bring forth better conditions so to improve each individual's existence. Only in unity can one reach their fullest potential. But distracted, and inevitably divided, all efforts are easily thwarted. This chapter introduces several of the beliefs that distract the people from higher intentions and realizing their underdeveloped disposition.

Disagreement over the Social Contract

As natural as the powers that be make the artificial seem, I didn't agree to the irrational cost to live, the low wages, an infant's purchasing power, the rich getting richer, a paycheque-to-paycheque requiem, the extinction of the savings account, a life on credit, sabotage of the social-net, high taxes, the death of the middle-class, corporate mass pollution, earthly destruction, disposable economics, genetic modifications, the feudal system manifest as a rental living and a life-long mortgage, the decay of democratic instruments, popular culture's challenge of moral standards, and on and on. If there is a choice, why would any person want the above regressive and exploitative happenings?

Standing in the hall of virtue and kindness, behind a podium constructed by the Great Spirit, proclaim I do that the Old World attitude is again prevalent. With the passing of each year, it becomes more and more dominant. I think it's safe to suggest that the needs of the general public call for a new agreement. Unless of course, the days of old, when kings and queens ruled, was best for the common person. During their reign over the people, humanity suffered on all levels, and the purpose of the people was to enrich and protect their status, wealth, and power—nothing less and nothing more. It was a time when the people economically, socially, spiritually, cognitively, and politically suffered.

To prevent a regression back to that type of civilization, behind Rawl's *Veil of Ignorance*, the public should revisit the contemporary **social contract**. The *Veil of Ignorance* is a hypothetical situation designed by John Rawl. The scenario asks that people, before making a decision able to impact a nation, step behind a veil, and there, strip themselves of their various dispositions. Behind the veil, all people are equal and all belong to the same caste. From this platform, on behalf of a nation's people, they make decisions. But how to convince the shepherds to parley with the sheep when the people are powerless and scrawny?

Insignificant is the people's strength—there isn't enough muscle to bring the shepherds to the table and negotiate. Tactfully, the general public are trained to stand as distracted individuals. This characteristic restrains the power of the people. Only in awareness and unity can we bargain for better living conditions.

Standing alone, and with little control over resources, those exploited by the contemporary social contract cannot take any meaningful action to change their realities. Nonetheless, I guess we can protest.

L.o.l.

Contemporary protests are useless and governments, corporations, and banks do what they want regardless. Countless protests later and the Old World attitude is still dragging the people back to a time before the Second World War, when the people of the planet suffered under the rule of robber-barons, super-wealthy families, kings, queens, trusts, and bankers. Regrettably, protests are useless unless enough people protest, and to change our social contract, everyone infected must mobilize and act. But this I cannot see happening anytime soon. Why? Well, the people are conditioned to stand as distracted individuals.

Until our individual ideologies incorporate a righteous collective consciousness, and until we stand together in a spirit of peace and non-compliance, to express our dissatisfaction with the many regressive happenings, we'll be stuck with an outdated social contract and the cycle of exploitation and hardship that comes with. This cycle the unborn will inherit.

Cage we do ourselves and cage we do the unborn—tomorrow's children will inherit the cycle we allow to continue and they'll face even greater hardship and exploitation. Unless of course, today's generation is willing to make the appropriate sacrifices and stand united. The power of the people is not a myth. Conquer we can the darkness. But before we can move in this direction, an understanding of what distracts and divides the general public is required. With this, *Distracted and Defeated* will help. Keep reading and you'll discover many of the tactics utilized to distract a person and divide each from the whole.

....

Some philosophers readily insinuate that by participating in contemporary society, an individual gives their consent to the shortcomings of society and her social contract. But I must ask—How is it a choice when born with no choice? No other choice there is. To eat, a person has no choice but to participate. However, if born with an AK in hand, fifty million in the bank, and the appropriate knowledge, a choice there would be.

History is a continuous battle between "the rulers" and "the ruled". No matter if "the ruled" think they're shepherds.

Near Defeat

When analyzing historical conflict, it becomes more than apparent, the catalyst of positive social change is the middle-class. But unfortunately, the contemporary middle-class is pre-occupied and distracted from wanting this change. Nor have they realized their traditional and unconventional responsibility.

And through no fault to them. The contemporary middle-class person is encouraged to farm wants without communal value. The person is encouraged to think he or she can rise above the status of a **middle-class peasant** and this as an individual. And the person is encouraged to want, chase, acquire, and enjoy material possessions, a selfish image, and sensory pleasure. In a nutshell, the middle-class individual is bred isolated from the whole and mothered by a culture that doesn't provide higher intention. Tragically, this can result in an underdeveloped human.

The game doesn't end there and when a person isn't distracted by the above, the contemporary middle-class mind is misdirected by the monthly bills, a credit score, and the eight hours of sweat daily exchanged for life's basics. After which, most are too tired to think about positive social change, let alone, want it. If time is idle, a person is more likely to escape the everyday stress by engaging in activities that require little thought such as fishing, dining out, drinking wine, playing cards, watching a movie, enjoying a sporting event, or interacting with a video game console.

Historically, the middle-class is the catalyst of positive social change, but unfortunately, **the machine** distracts the contemporary middle-class mind from thoughts with benevolent and collective intention. As such, the middle-class has forgotten. Moreover, the distractions and hardships have existed for so long that they appear to originate from the dominion of nature and her principles—akin to afternoon sunshine or dirt beneath the feet, and not from the manmade reality.

But even if the middle-class were to realize beautiful and benevolent intentions, it's fairly clear that the cost of living has reached an irrational level—especially in the category of housing. It's also clear that wages didn't keep up with this growth—drastically shrinking the savings account. What this means is, the middle-class has and is losing purchasing power. In turn, the middle-class has and is losing the financial power to challenge and change the things in need of change.

The march to the battlefield is uphill from here, and with the passing of every generation, the climb will grow steeper. As the generations pass, the hardships that hinder positive change will only increase in strength.

When analyzing historical conflict, it becomes more than apparent that the catalyst of positive social change is the middle-class. But unfortunately, the contemporary middle-class is pre-occupied and distracted from wanting this change. Nor have they realized their traditional and unconventional responsibility.

....

Although no theatre of positive change is without the middle-class, the hands of change are always the destitute. The hands of change typically arise from poor socio-economic conditions. But without the direction, the knowledge, and the resources of the middle-class, the hands of change are unlikely to succeed in creating and sustaining a positive transformation.

Like pawns on a life-size chessboard, the people are strategically moved about by those who rule, and they're moved about to maintain and enhance the status of the pieces with more value.

The Old is New

North America was meant to be the New World. A land envisioned as a place for the common person to live free of the corrupt influences perpetuated by the Old. And in the beginning, that was probably so, but on the contemporary scene, the Old World has infiltrated the New. Those who rule are again manipulating and exploiting the general public so to reinforce the status of the few. The bewildered herd must be controlled and society is structured to keep the people senselessly occupied and trapped as the ruled. Escape I wish for, as those who braved the New World not too long ago, but where to go? The Old are the masters of almost all.

Under the setting of the Old World, most people existed for the benefit of the wealthiest, and the structure of society, including the beliefs taught to the general public, were designed to reinforce the power of that group. Yet, the contemporary person doesn't know what was meant by the term, and with few to defend the vision of a New World, the Old attitude slowly seeped back into the picture. Understand my friend, civilization is taking steps backward.

Decoding Life

A person is forced to chase their basic needs, each person is pitted against each in their chase, and most people are unable to secure their basics for a protracted period.

I'm a little confused. I thought people entered into a social contract so to create better living conditions. In which, an individual is able to secure the basics for a prolonged period of time. I thought that markets and societies came to be to assist a person harness his or her potential and to the heavens climb.

Perhaps, that was true in the beginning, but on the contemporary scene, most individuals are unaware why the people of the past entered into a social contract. And ironically, contemporary markets and societies are more able than ever to provide the basics to all people without a person having to bust their back, or exchange their mind for a paycheque-to-paycheque lifestyle.

As it is, under the current economic circumstances, most people are not permitted to financially climb and only sanctioned to maintain a bi-weekly existence. Friends, our social contract must be reassessed. That is, if we wish to gift the unborn a higher and truer standard of living.

The contemporary human being is hurting and tomorrow's children will hurt even more, and the person suffers as any organism living in an environment conducive not to survival. To cope with the dissonance, tens-of-millions of North Americans are popping narcotics—such as anti-depressants, sleeping pills, and/or anti-psychotics. And tens-of-millions more spend their evenings and weekends intoxicated.

The modern person suffers because the world built by the rulers isn't harmonized with the human. The two, like oil and water, are not blending. But yet, so many assent. Perhaps, it's because those drugged-up or intoxicated have little cognitive strength, and the rest are too busy to allow their thoughts to fly and see the world through the eyes of a hawk.

Through the view of a bird in flight, the dissension is hard to miss, like the Nazca Lines in South Peru, or the nation shaped as a boot. Looking down on the workings of society, it's apparent, and the manmade world isn't helping the person progress. Instead, it unnecessarily causes the human stress. But again, those infected reluctantly acquiesce. Quietly, each sets aside their humanity and bows before the shepherds.

....

The high cost of living, especially in housing, is an artificial happening and it curbs the amount of money the middle-class accumulate. Some suggest that this is purposely so because, after the Second World War, the middle-class accumulated too much wealth, in particular, immigrants, and they were able to demand positive change from corporations and governments. However, the current and ridiculous cost of living has effectively changed all of that.

For over the past few decades, the cost of living has annually grown a few percent. Simultaneously, the amount of money the average person takes home didn't keep up with that growth. Since the 1980s, the cost of living has increased by over 130%, and on average, wages increased less than 10% of that. To add, the people are saving approximately 1% of their income (9% less than a few decades back), and several million households have no savings. Naturally, less money typically leads to more debt, and over the past thirty years, debt has increased at an annual rate of about 5%, and almost all people are indebted.

If not for a line of credit, how many people would make it to the next paycheque? Debt-slaves most people are and few bother to challenge the low wages and the high cost to live. I guess they're comfortable in their prison cells, or they haven't realized that they're imprisoned. Friends, recognize, there is more to human existence.

Financial stress limits a person's awareness, like the blinders on a racehorse, or out-of-focus prescription glasses.

Bread and Circuses

The Ancient Roman rulers, so to maintain power and control over the Roman people, employed a strategy known as "bread and circuses".

The term "bread" refers to the tactic of deprivation. If a person is constantly thinking about or working toward securing their financial and physiological needs, he or she will be easier to control. Nor will an individual have the time or energy to think about ideas and actions able to improve their existence as a human.

The term "circuses" denotes amusements and entertainment. If a person's downtime, when he or she isn't thinking about or working toward securing their physiological needs, is preoccupied by "circuses," an individual will not realize their exploitative existence. Likewise, a person will not have an opportunity to envision a less oppressive situation. The easy pleasures made available to the Roman public were designed to distract an individual from conceptualizing higher intentions.

"Bread and circuses" are effective tools to maintain control. Moreover, "bread" is an excellent means to gain popular support and to convince a person to soldier. Most hungry people will compromise moral standards to feed the self, and when the ruling class wish to war, they exploit this weakness. Killers are required by most nations so to grow and to survive, but how many individuals will murder another human being if his or her existence didn't depend on it?

Deprivation and distraction were tools used by Ancient Roman rulers, and if you examine the movements of the contemporary person, those tools are again in use.

By way of a paycheque-to-paycheque existence, a mortgaged living, a life on credit, and the irrationally high cost to exist, deprivation is common. As the ancient Roman people, few individuals have the financial security to think about more than survival. As mentioned, if a person's long-term prosperity, security, and potential to meet the basics are constantly under threat, as they are for most modern individuals, the mind will do little but think about alleviating that threat or the mind will stress about it. This type of mindset naturally limits a person's awareness and it typically collapses onto itself. (For more detail to how the people are financially deprived, please read a previous publication, *A Beautiful Destruction*).

Tactics of deprivation and distraction are in play, but unlike Roman chariot races, public executions, and gladiator matches, the modern means and methods able to sidetrack the herd are far more advanced. Today, things such as television programs, sports, concerts, celebrities, gossip magazines, and "special days" like Valetine's Day are employed.

Ancient Roman tactics are used to misdirect the general public. Most people are unaware of the restricting disposition. And tragically, it doesn't end with "bread and circuses". The intelligence of a person is tampered with in many other ways. As you'll discover in the upcoming articles.

....

Forces were already in play, power struggles were already staged, and a person is born in the game without knowing how it's actually played.

The many branches of popular media, such as radio and television, are tools employed by the ruling class to distract the general public. Used they are like weapons.

Dead Heroes and Gangsters

When it's not the financial stress or the circuses, emotions are provoked so to distract.

You see, occasionally and purposely, emotions such as fear and sympathy are played with to pre-occupy and distract an individual from higher thoughts and greater ends. Emotions are tickled through the stories and rumours of terrorists, economic recessions, dead heroes, health risks, gangsters, crooked politicians, rescued orphans, and on and on.

As Sun Tzu suggested, misdirect the enemy and then engage, and the people, through their individual emotions, are constantly diverted from courting thoughts able to challenge the things that require change.

A very effective war tactic it is, and the mind is distracted while the exploitation, year after year, continues to worsen. The emotions misdirect an individual and behave as a smokescreen. Behind the smoke, the contemporary kings and queens of the world plunder and transfer more and more hardship to society.

When it's not the financial stress or the circuses, emotions are provoked so to distract.

"To repress rebellion is to maintain the status quo, a condition which binds the mortal creature in a state of intellectual or physical slavery. But it is impossible to chain man merely by slaving his body; the mind also must be held, and to accomplish this, fear is the accepted weapon. The common man must fear life, fear death, fear God, fear the Devil, and fear most the overlords, the keepers of his destiny." — Manly P. Hall

To Believe

Most of what a person knows of the self and the world around him or her did not accompany the individual out from the womb. Knowledge is handed-down by the manmade world and most of what an individual knows is learned. The two dominant sources that hand-down information are the popular culture and the collective intelligence.

The collective intelligence is constituted by the ideas, beliefs, wants, and knowledge most people have in common. The collective intelligence is typically transferred generation to generation; changing to reflect the changes that occur within the popular culture.

Popular culture can be understood as the dominant ideas, beliefs, wants, and knowledge the contemporary market and government propagate. If the popular culture is effectively communicated to the general public, the values housed by the popular culture will merge with the collective intelligence.

In the type of world we live in, most of what an individual knows is taught by the two heads mentioned. Outside those two are few teachers and they do not have near the same influence. Unfortunately, both the heads are failing to supply the substance required to comprehend the complete picture of the human existence.

Artificial Inflation

Not all the beliefs perpetuated by popular culture and the collective intelligence are designed to help improve a person's existence, and ideas such as racism and sexism are handed-down by the establishment so to divide each from each. And of course, to mislead those who weren't "ismed" into believing they have it good and their situation might worsen if the status quo changes.

Beliefs are fiddled with and it doesn't begin and end with the two above examples. The rabbit hole is deep. Not much is off limits. And tragically, one of the greatest human weaknesses is subject to exploitation. In the campaign to misdirect a person's thoughts and intentions, the sexual impulse is tampered with.

Conditioned and reinforced by the popular messages delivered through tools as television, pop music, mainstream magazines, and big-budget films, popular culture encourages promiscuity amid the sexes and artificially inflates the sex drive.

Popular culture appears to influence a person's value system to center their existence on the pursuit of sexual pleasure and not higher development—whoring is positioned as socially acceptable. In this endeavour, gender relations are muddied and people view the opposite sex more for their pleasure properties and not their character.

Likewise, sexual restraint is no longer associated with ideas of honour, virtue, and high character, and intimacy is no longer associated with sex. Moreover, women and men are both encouraged to pursue sexual pleasure without the emotional and spiritual commitment. As a result, people actually pride themselves on their unrestrained behaviour, and many understand the pursuit of sexual pleasure as purposeful as feeding the self.

The state of mind popular culture attempts to mould doesn't benefit the person, and it distracts the mind from higher intentions and conceptualizing a less exploitative existence.

Not only that, an artificially inflated sex drive can induce a person to accidentally blur the line between lust and love. A couple who've confused the two, and who are not cognitively compatible, can cause each other suffering. That is, when the two aren't pleasing their sexual attractions. You see, the confusion between lust and love can coerce a person to maintain an unhealthy relationship and troop through the suffering each causes. Or the two will eventually realize their incompatibility and separate. But sometimes, before this happens, they create an offspring. The confusion between lust and love has left some children at a disadvantage—they're raised by one biological parent. The confusion has also damaged the minds of those who've separated. A separation from a long-term relationship can induce pain. The withdrawal from neural pathways, centered on one's partner, is similar to a heroin addict of a decade in rehabilitation—stuck in a cycle of thoughts that perpetually distract a person.

An inflated sex drive further gives rise to the "the player" attitude. This state of mind encourages the host to value members of the opposite sex strictly for their pleasure properties and to sample as many as possible—regardless the harm done to another human being. When "the player" is on the hunt for sexual satisfaction, he or she doesn't comprehend or recognize another's conscious existence, and if a member of the opposite sex does fall prey to the lust of "the player", afterward, they'll probably suffer. The suffering is a natural outcome, and the pain and depressive state brought about by "the player" can be short-term to lifelong.

Many negative consequences accompany the artificial and inflated depiction of sex by popular culture. Within the context of this manuscript, the unrealistic representation, and the consequences of the fabrication, provide another means of misdirecting the minds of the people. Since the sexual drive is one of the most powerful motivators housed by a person, the manipulation is one of the most powerful tactics employed by the rulers.

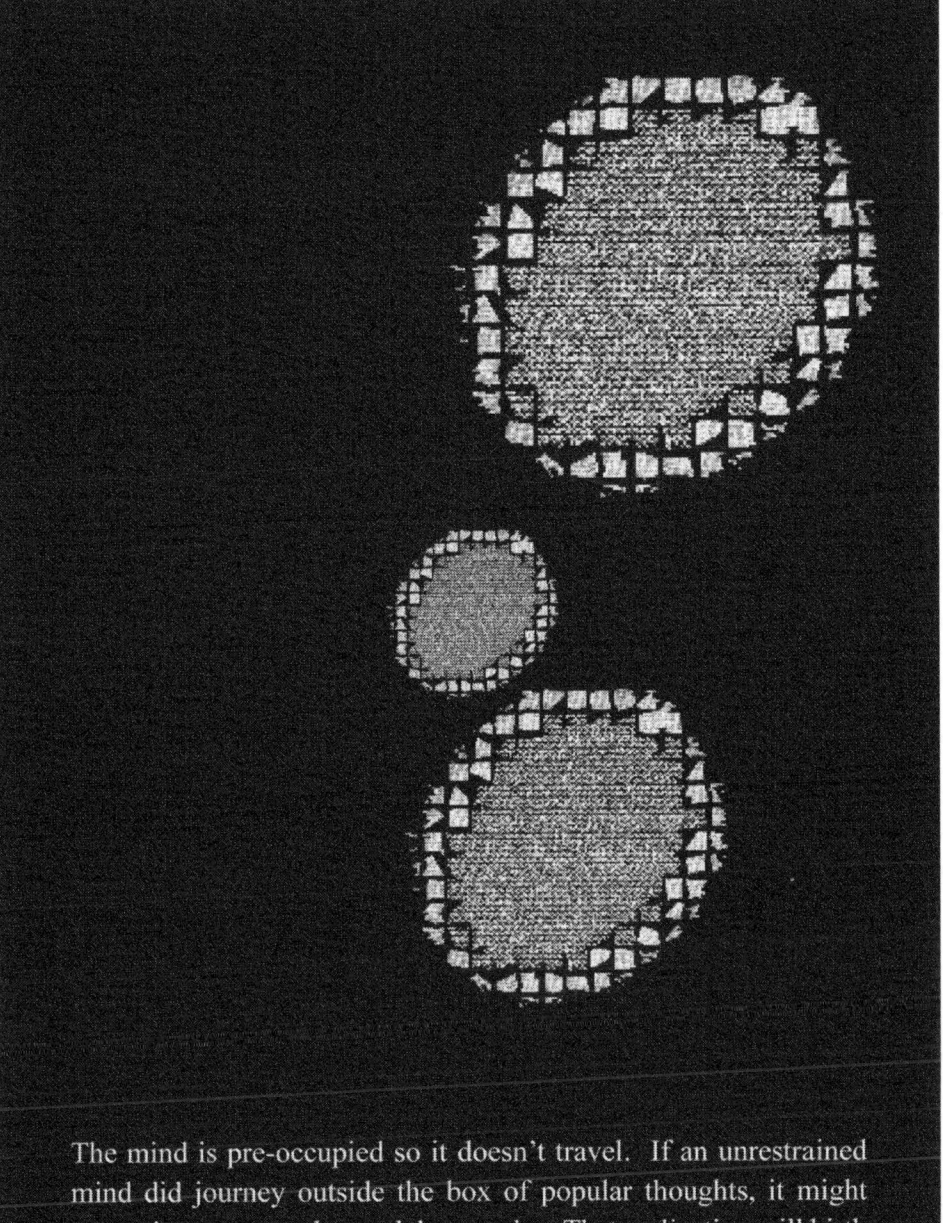

The mind is pre-occupied so it doesn't travel. If an unrestrained mind did journey outside the box of popular thoughts, it might recognize a purpose beyond the popular. That realization will birth a craving for better living conditions—so to fulfill a higher purpose. This yearning naturally challenges the rule of the shepherds.

The Big O

The sex drive is artificially inflated and the "Big O" isn't placed within the proper setting. But again, this all makes sense. The Big O is a source of immense energy, and when harnessed, it's able to gift the mind and body with Herculean strength.

Nonetheless, even if it isn't harnessed, the mind and body still require it to optimally function, and when the Big O is released, the mind and body no longer have access to essential energy and the person's vitality suffers. A person becomes much slower and weaker in mind and body—he or she is not as sharp, not as quick, not as clever, not as intelligent, and not as aware. In such a state, a person will not fully understand complex ideas, and the notions and motions that trap the sheep to the caste of the ruled are very complicated. A sharp mind is required to understand them.

The sex drive is artificially inflated and the Big O isn't placed within the proper setting. Instead, the general public are encouraged to release it as often as they can. This naturally weakens a person and a frail individual is much easier to control than one with Herculean strength.

....

Not only do the mind and body suffer when the Big O is released, as does a person's spiritual potential. Only by harnessing the power of the Big O can an individual's spirit progress.

Pleasure-Seekers

When it isn't the bread, when it isn't the circuses, pleasure misdirects the mind from higher awareness.

Sensory satisfaction is a natural thing but the chase for and the acquisition of is encouraged to speak without need, and frequently. Too often, pleasure is valued before higher meaning.

Abstinence

Demonically and successfully, popular culture persuades many individuals that abstinence isn't the social standard, and the most influential, pre-adults, readily believe that losing one's virginity is a high life value.

Popular culture no longer associates virginity with honour, virtue, and self-respect. But instead, with popularity, the good life, and social acceptance. People are led to believe that "virginity" is a label that should be alleviated as quickly as possible.

As if possessed but most likely misled, people are also taught to reinforce the artificially injected belief amongst each other. Every other person seems to propagate that losing one's virginity is a high life value.

Surprisingly, the popular idea of love can also distract, preoccupy, and numb a person's mind as sex, fear, finances, and bread can.

Love as a Distraction

Love for and from another person, and the chase to secure it, is showcased as a high life purpose—regardless of how poor one might be, their status as a debt-slave, the obstacles that prevent their self-actualization (enlightenment), and the occasional corrupt behaviour of governments, banks, and corporations. Our popular culture has convinced most people that the artificial hardships and abasement are "okay" so long as a person has love for and from another person.

The individual is tricked. He and she is deceived to believe that all man-induced hardships are bearable, so long as there's love for and from another human.

Don't get me wrong, love is all good. Love is all good so long as the chemical induction doesn't distract, preoccupy, or numb a person's mind from developing ideas, beliefs, and wants of higher value, and from analyzing and challenging the artificial hardships most people suffer under. A love that distracts, preoccupies, and numbs is a love that imprisons the person and a life behind bars isn't a life lived.

To add to the premeditated illusion, love has another jagged edge and a lover without love is like an alcoholic without booze—a person is in a state of withdrawal. Prolonged exposure to a particular stimulant creates neural pathways, and when those chemical pathways are not given attention by the stimulation which created them, the mind produces the sensations of suffering—anger, sadness, depression, anxiety, and/or rumination. That type of cognitive condition naturally limits a person's awareness.

It doesn't end there, not only can the loss of love, and the love for and from, cage a person's awareness, as can the chase for the chemical configuration. In the search for love, sometimes, a person can become so overly consumed with the chase that their mind thinks of little else.

Love for and from another person, and the chase to secure it, is presented as a high life purpose. However, the chemical configuration can sometimes distract, preoccupy, and numb the mind from higher thoughts and a better existence. But again, don't get me wrong, love is all good. Love is all good so long as it doesn't morph into a cognitive prison.

Soulmate

Movies and music have convinced almost every person that he or she is incomplete, and only another human being can complete him or her. However, a person is born whole and doesn't require another person to complete their human condition. More specifically, movies and music suggest that the soul is incomplete and it requires another soul to be whole—a soulmate. But the soul is born intact and movies and music are misleading the person.

So to further distract a person, an individual is deceived to believe that he or she must search for another to be whole. But how can a missing half to something that's complete ever be found? This deception runs deep, and for generations, the people have chased the beast.

The Art of Mating

An unbeneficial coupling can occur. This can happen if the two in the relationship do not understand the nature of love and the art of mating.

There are guidelines to the art of mating, but those who rule countries hide this knowledge from the common person. Perhaps, it's because this knowledge might empower the sheep, their offspring, their children's progeny, and on and on.

The art of mating is simple. A choice in a partner is less influenced by chemical inductions and considerations such as a person's genetics, family lineage, financial strength, level of education, mental stability, spiritual potency, and knowledge of the physical and invisible worlds are the priorities. Selecting a mate for other reasons than chemical inductions is important. That is, if a person's goal is to become more than a member of the ruled class. In this endeavour, large amounts of cash, a well-built network of the right people, knowledge, spiritual strength, and mental stability are a must. But the art of mating isn't taught by our popular culture. As such, most people overlook the above considerations and silently take their place amid the herd—simultaneously trapping the yet born.

Children born into a family unit, managed by people who do not adhere to the principles of mating, come into this world with shackles around the head, hands, torso, and feet. Born they are at a disadvantage—born they are as screws for the system—born they are to constantly desire an escape from this human experiment. They were defeated before they even took birth because their parents didn't understand the art of mating.

An unbeneficial coupling can occur. This can happen if the two in the relationship do not understand the nature of love and the art of mating.

Liquor, Nicotine, and Things

Choices do increase an individual's freedom of mind, yet, uninformed choices can limit an individual's freedom of thought. For example, such things as liquor, nicotine, pornography, and gambling can create a powerful dependence (a cognitive attachment manifest by way of neural-pathways). A dependent mind defines its reality centered on the agent(s) it's attached to. Such a state of mind isn't free to experience, to choose, or to explore. And such a state of mind isn't the master of thoughts, wants, and choices, but is instead a servant and determined.

If such things as liquor, nicotine, pornography, and gambling are to be lawful and a social norm, then the system should also educate every individual about them and their potential to limit a person's awareness. In addition, it might be important to teach people how the limitations might be broken.

The potential for the aforementioned to create a dependent person isn't a new understanding. Most of the decision-makers were and are aware of the potential. They weren't and aren't slow on the uptake. However, ask yourself—Why haven't they removed such choices if they're unwilling to teach an individual how to master such things, so they do not master the person? Why did and do they foster the stuff that cultivates a servant?

Could it be that a dependent mind is in their benefit? Maybe, a dependent mind is easier to distract than one not so dependent? Perhaps, a dependent mind is a requirement before the elite can plunder, exploit, and thicken the invisible chains?

....

"Man is born free; and everywhere he is in chains. One thinks himself the master of others, and still remains a greater slave than they." — Jean-Jacques Rousseau

Alcohol and Disunity

It's no secret and alcohol can cause a human being to suffer.   Moreover, the substance also induces disunity amid a people.

Alcohol paves the way for disunity by pushing the wicked within a person out. Most adults have witnessed the dark consequences of the substance. Those consequences feed disunity amongst the masses.   Yet, liquor is sanctioned as socially and legally acceptable. Surprisingly, some religious institutions also openly endorse the use of the potion.

I'm a little baffled. Why would the powers that be allow for a substance proven as a cause of dissonance?   I thought the powers that be were working to improve the living standards of a nation's people. That's the message they've pushed for decades upon decades upon decades.

The powers that be not only allow for the dissonance, they also popularizing the potion. This is done by injecting specific values into our popular culture and our collective intelligence. Using techniques as "third party comments" and "third party examples", the use of alcohol is associated with such things as relaxing, sporting, socializing, celebrating, and a person's free time. Alcohol is associated as such so to influence a person to consider alcohol as socially acceptable and an attribute of a normal lifestyle.

The term, third party comment, is a technique able to persuade a person of a particular belief. The technique involves other people speaking positively about the belief you wish to communicate. This technique is often used in movies. For example, to create a reputation, and to develop how the audience will perceive a specific character, the writer of a movie will script supporting characters to comment on the perception the writer wishes to build. If the writer would like the audience to think of a character as a gifted guitarist, the writer will employ other characters to comment on this talent. Perhaps, the supporting characters will talk about the different awards he's won or at what age he first picked-up a guitar.

A third party example is an instance of the idea you wish to instil. If attempting to influence people to interact a certain way when in a certain situation, give examples of individuals behaving in that manner. Moreover, create a positive aura to compliment the illustration.

It's no secret and alcohol can cause a human being to suffer. Moreover, the substance also induces disunity amid a people. However, the powers that be see fit to popularize the substance. Can it be that the normalization is another trick to keep the people under control, in the status quo, and defeated?

Individuality

The idea of an individual, who makes autonomous decisions, is a myth but it's presented as an absolute so to misdirect.

If you don't believe me, answer this—What's so unique about absorbing information that every mind uses to create wants and values? It's not as if you're the only one who watches the television, listens to the radio, surfs the internet, reads the newspaper, and attended public school.

I ask—What uniqueness do you exercise when you're built with the same innate wants that everyone is built with? You too hunger, thirst, and desire to belong.

I ask—What's so unique when the popular culture and the collective intelligence induce the same behaviour and habits in all people? What's so unique about wanting what everyone wants—large amounts of cash, a few vehicles, status, respect, and a summer cottage?

I ask—What uniqueness do you exercise when each does as everyone else? So to fit in, you too chase a nine-to-five, the basics, the bills, a line of credit, a mortgage, entertainment, and the other elements of the accepted image?

They say that you and I can be individuals? They say that you and I have a uniqueness that we can exercise? They say... They say... They say... And I think they say to distract and divide.

....

A lone wolf who doesn't know how to run with the pack, and thinks his or her bite is greater than, sacrifices the fruits of a united front.

A False Notion of Success

The contemporary person's beliefs and wants are limited and the person is unaware of this. You see, beliefs and wants are manipulated so a person will maintain and enhance the status quo and not challenge it—nothing more and nothing less. Unaware, the mind is restricted from a higher state of realization and the mind operates within a limited framework.

Beliefs and wants are tampered with so to keep the divisions within society as is. To further prevent the individual from realizing the deception, the engineered beliefs and wants are presented as the best options available to a person. For example, this notion of competing amongst each other, instead of standing together to improve human subsistence, is propagated as an optimal choice when in fact it isn't. The competition for power, wealth, and status amid the herd actually contributes to the lack of progress.

The modern person, as the ancient Roman, is pitted against their neighbour and forced to fight other human begins for the necessities of life. Because of this occurrence, another falsehood is brought about. Sometimes, those who've escaped a paycheque-to-paycheque reality think they've conquered the world. Not realizing the bigger picture, not realizing the real battle, but satisfied with winning the fight for what is rightfully theirs.

But I guess this attitude is understandable. A person who's lived with little money, for a prolonged period of time, can develop an idea of success within limits and a counterfeit notion of achievement can be had—a person can grow to harbour a **false consciousness**. Perhaps, this false notion of success is so because of the proposed life purposes. The ruled are told that accumulating material means, chasing money, having the latest thing, consuming without need, a mortgaged living, a nine-to-five until after the age of sixty, and acquiring some sort of status—able to distinguish a person from the other humans, are the reasons an individual exists on this planet. Moreover, the person is taught to believe, by accomplishing the proposed purposes, they've fulfilled their obligation to the self, their fellow humans, the planet, the future generations, and The Great Architect. Under this false sense of accomplishment, a person will likely spend the remainder of their life pleasing the senses.

This inaccurate depiction of success encourages the people to feel satisfaction without having touched true accomplishments. Their norms of reality are trapped to a limited perspective, and consumed by the ego, they rest when they should be fulfilling the obligations of every middle-class citizen. Unwittingly, they initiate the generations under them to the same deception that imprisons their thoughts and actions.

This notion of success, and the life purposes associated to it, misdirect the energy of the woman and man. Many people spend their entire life believing they're working toward something of value but, in the grand scheme of things, they aren't. Yet, this attitude is understandable. A person who's lived with little money, for a prolonged period of time, can develop an idea of success within limits.

....

People are taught to think they can be shepherds, but with little ways and means, sheep remain sheep and eventually die of broken dreams. It's a cycle of melancholy, and without knowing it, under the impression of a life purpose and chasing a false notion, a person only lynches their happiness.

Many individuals in the Western World think they're free, but almost all are enslaved to currency. A person can only entertain the idea of freedom after they're master of money. Freedom beforehand is simply an illusion. A debt-slave I am.

Sheep Make Sheep

A question for the ears of the Universe—Without a million in a bank account or buried in the backyard, isn't it cruel to birth a child? I only ask this because, at times, it seems as if life is given to a servant, born to suffer and struggle. All in the name of satisfying the system. Born to parents without large amounts of cash, a child only grows to repeat the same cycle that chains most parents—to work until grey and weak, to consume without need, to be told what to do and think, to sacrifice the spirit for material things, to pay an irrational price, and to bear the title "debt-slave".

It would appear, at times, the only thing most people give life to is a screw for the system, destined to endure, and this in so-called developed nations. The right to raise a child correctly is stolen by our artificial and destitute eco-political conditions. Escape I want from this experiment. Escape I want for myself and those yet to receive a body dependent. Is it possible to rewrite our social contract, or are these truly the best gifts we can leave tomorrow's children?

But not enough people are asking the right questions, and the **collective intelligence** convinces almost all people to create offspring as soon as a person stabilizes their income. Consideration isn't given to the world the unborn will be born to and their occupation as screws.

Without a million in a bank account or buried in the backyard, a person is simply a screw for the system, and under the guise of a life purpose, people give life to servants.

The human is more than a tiny chemical thing, on a planet blue and green, in a galaxy amongst billions. Can someone please tell those who rule the world.? Perhaps, if they know, they'll treat the individual as more than a screw for the system.

Popular culture teaches most people that life is a fluke, ape is their ancestor, and death is the end. This narrative strips a person of a higher meaning to existence. Simultaneously, the people are indoctrinated to think that meaning can only be found in the consumption of the material. From birth, most people are tricked to ignore the human potential.

Gears and Grease

A person's value system guides their thoughts and actions. As already mentioned, the value system can be tampered with. A person can be guided to harbour specific beliefs, wants, ideas, and expectations. To that effect, for the system to maintain its power, the people must never stop selfishly wanting more, and for the system to grow, the selfish wanting can never discontinue.

The gears of the machine must be continuously greased so they don't seize. As such, the system readily, and now effortlessly, compels a person's value system to pursue sensory pleasures, entertainment, a hand-me-down image, shiny things, the latest of the latest gadget, and on and on. Stuck they are in the consumer's bubble. Stuck they are as self-centered individuals.

The market has successfully injected the value system wanted by it, and now, the collective intelligence actually reinforces and propagates the value system created by the market. Moreover, the mentality of the herd marginalizations those who conform not to the collective intelligence.

The machine successfully persuades a person that the motions required to maintain the status quo are the most purposeful movements an individual can engage in. Unfortunately, the way things are only enriches the masters of the market and exploits the rest.

From childhood, almost all people are tricked to think of the artificial and fleeting purposes and wants as an absolute like the moon. Under this illusion, a better existence is the sacrifice.

The Chase

The race for such things as a career, a spouse, 2.5 kids, a mortgage, a retirement savings plan, and so on, are presented as absolute purposes with none higher. Yet, higher meaning there is.

I guess the chase for the mentioned is desirable, but in the modern age, the chase consumes too much of a person's daily energy and time. Little of the two remain after a nine-to-five. With minimal energy and time, how can an individual possibly harness the heights of the spirit, body, and mind? My troublesome nature is having a difficult go at accepting this. My indigo mind can't process the purpose of existing if not reaching for heights.

"What good fortune for those in power that people do not think." — Adolf Hitler

How They Do It

To infuse a belief within a person, an individual must construct a positive connotation pertaining to that value. To this end, for a person to construct a belief, an individual requires access to enough diverse and relevant information. In addition, all opposing values must be discredited. For a person to believe in a value, he or she mustn't be able to justify any opposing view.

There are two methods of introducing a belief, either by directly communicating the idea or by indirectly communicating it.

Some people aren't very critical and they'll believe almost any idea, so long as the notion is presented by a trusted source and in a trustworthy manner. However, some people are critical and they don't like to be told what 1 and 1 equals. Instead, they prefer to discover the answer for themselves. For those types of people, the idea must be communicated in a way that allows a person to believe they reasoned independently. If people believe they used their own abilities to reach an end, they're more likely to accept that end and to incorporate it into their value system.

To indirectly communicate an idea:

- •Inject subtle comments within movies, television sitcoms, and talk shows.
- •Publish articles in newspapers and publish books.
- •Influence the televised newscast.
- •Create academically supported arguments.

•Hire well-received people as spokespeople to push the idea.

•Create third-party examples.

•Design and perpetuate third-party comments.

•Create sub-organizations to sell the message.

•Associate the idea to a human emotion or to a person's selfish wants.

•Associate the idea to the human condition's innate wants.

•Associate the idea to a person's fears such as death.

•And/or associate the idea to an existing popular and positive idea such as freedom or God.

It should be noted that all the information an individual absorbs, subconsciously influences him or her. Sometimes, it's enough to bombard a person's mind with information so to convince him or her of a particular viewpoint, and sometimes, it's enough to bombard a person's mind with personified examples of the belief.

The same indirect techniques mentioned above can also discredit an idea. Instead of presenting an idea in a positive setting as you would the idea you wish to sell, add a negative spin to it. For example, when the idea is discussed in public, have the speakers roll their eyes and have them associate the idea with terms akin to "primitive" and "evil".

Once the desired idea has existed long enough to penetrate the cultural collective intelligence, the collective intelligence, and its environmental counterparts, will slowly do the work of indoctrinating a people to a particular idea. Once the suggestion is adopted as popular, the people will reinforce the idea and expect it from other people, and more importantly, from those yet born.

For the most part, the first generation of people exposed to the new belief might fight it, especially if the idea is inaccurate and if they already have an accurate depiction. But the following generations will more easily accept the belief. That is, if the idea is successfully injected into the collective intelligence. People born to a particular popular idea are less likely to challenge it. They'll likely perceive the idea as natural as a raindrop or a snowflake.

Master and Servant

The reality we live in is artificially inflated and it conditions far too many untruthful and unrealistic wants, beliefs, ideas, and expectations. For this reason, the space and time in the place of thinking is too busy—there's little room for higher living. All the while, real needs receive little attention, those like true freedom, true happiness, true belonging, the "true me", true peace, and true relations.

A limited awareness is indoctrinated and most people digest it. But what other choice is there? An individual becomes the environment, and in today's world, the environment grooms the master as servant and alienates the "I" from knowing what it is to be master of wants, beliefs, ideas, and expectations. Inevitably and unknowingly, a person restricts their own human experience.

To Want

We were designed to have wants. It's as natural as winter and fall. However, not all wants are born with us and most wants are limited constructs—given by our environments—designed to guide us and create compliance.

This to ensure the supply-lines stay unravelled. This to ensure collective thought doesn't travel. Wants constructed unguided can be unpredictable. Unwanted change can occur. The people might want more. Imagine a built world complimentary of the human creature.

Many popular wants and beliefs are unable to help a person realize their full potential. But constantly looking for the cheese, and stuck inside a maze, it's a phantasm difficult to comprehend and rise above.

To Repeat

Trained we've been to repeat ideas and not to examine and to generate. But I guess this makes sense. If we were taught to examine the "truths" asserted by the artificial world, we might realize the limited nature of the assertions and generate reasonable alternatives. Alternatives that challenge the status quo. Reasonable alternatives have the potential to better the people's living standard. But reasonable options also attack those who benefit from the way things are.

Reasonable alternatives are missed because most people are too busy repeating and not generating ideas able to levitate the human experience. We're all guilty of it, and since the human being becomes the information it gathers from the world, it's difficult to escape the phenomenon.

This all said, Repeaters are an asset to those who benefit from the current state of affairs, and they help to maintain and to reinforce how things are. Oh, and Repeaters help to indoctrinate the newly born. Consider the Repeater a member of an enslaved people, who helps the masters maintain their oppressive control and immoral disciplinary power. The pinnacle of which are middle-management and the other professionals such as teachers and professors. They don't financially suffer as most people do and they don't suffer so they'll support the status quo. You see, they're given enough to curb their afflictions and thus they don't challenge. Furthermore, their unfamiliarity with the financial hardships of most people convinces them that the structure of the eco-political platform must be solid for all, just as it is for them. However, they too are members of the ruled class and they too are stuck in the same matrix that all the sheep are trapped in. The only difference is, they're most able of the ruled to change the world. They have the finances and the network to make it so. But until they realize their standing, they're nothing more than sheepdogs, loyal to the shepherds. Without them, the sheep are near-impossible to herd.

Trained we've been to repeat ideas and not to examine and to generate. But I guess this makes sense. If we were taught to examine the "truths" asserted by the artificial world, we might realize the limited nature of the assertions and generate reasonable alternatives.

"Most people are other people. Their thoughts are someone else's opinions, their lives a mimicry, their passions a quotation." — Oscar Wilde

Provocateur

Self-helpers and motivational speakers are like an Uncle Tom. That is, so long as they try and convince the people to change and not the eco-political system which shelters the causes of their economic, social, and political suffering.

Uncle Toms they are and agents of the machine they be, and tragically, most of them think otherwise and they believe they're uplifting humanity. But in actuality, they're further indoctrinating their fellow human beings, and instead of motivating people to see the chains placed by contemporary society, they try and make a person feel better about their inhuman disposition—slavery to a nine-to-five, a mortgaged life, a credit score, the extortion at the banks, a paycheque-to-paycheque requiem, and on and on.

Self-helpers and motivational speakers are like an Uncle Tom. That is, so long as they try and convince the people to change and not the eco-political system which shelters the causes of their economic, social, and political suffering.

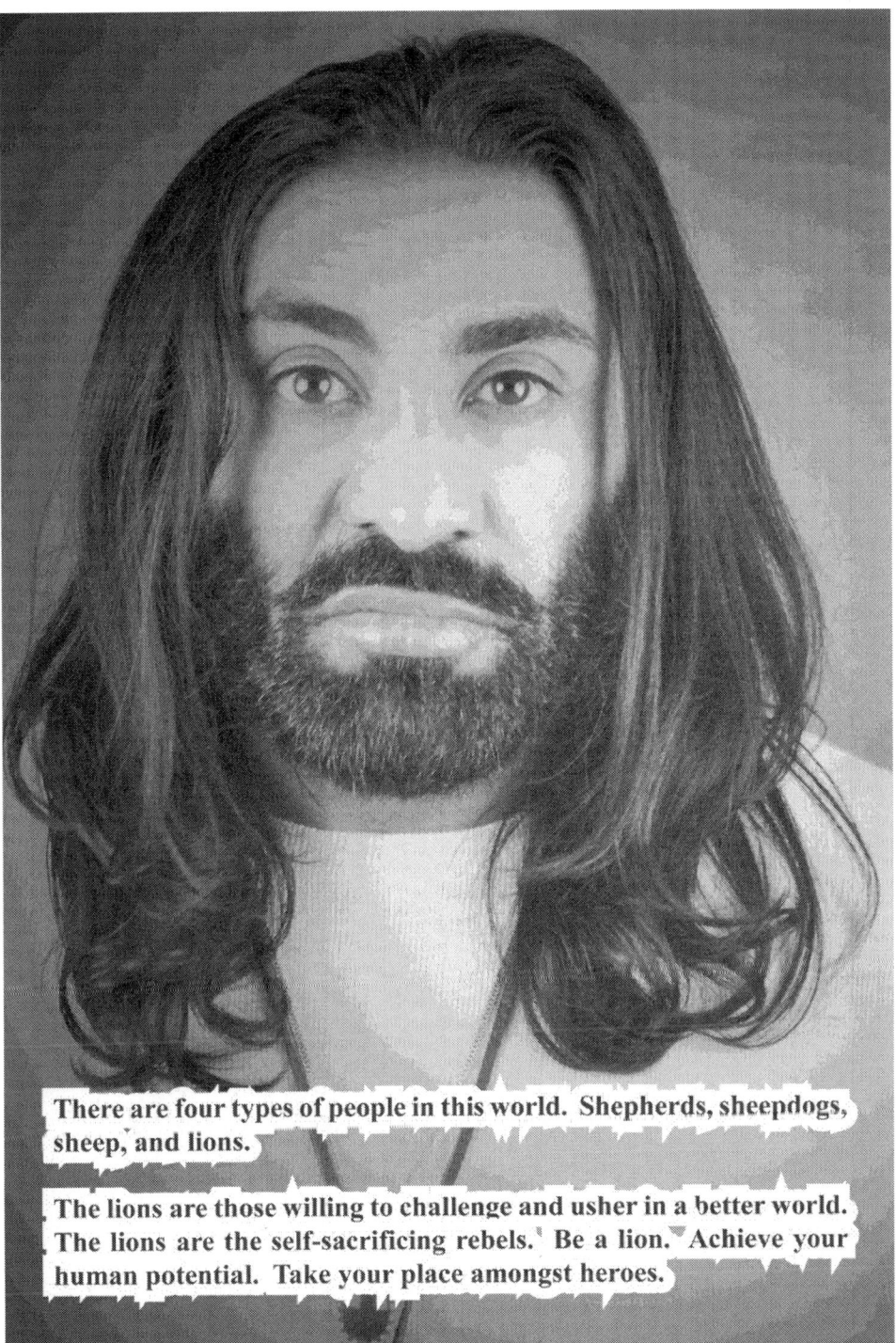

There are four types of people in this world. Shepherds, sheepdogs, sheep, and lions.

The lions are those willing to challenge and usher in a better world. The lions are the self-sacrificing rebels. Be a lion. Achieve your human potential. Take your place amongst heroes.

To Submit

I think most people eventually realize that the popular ideas such as a nine-to-five, endless consumption, a credit score, and a mortgaged existence aren't absolute. I think most people eventually reach the conclusion that there must be more to the human experience.

I also believe that by the time a person breaks through the social constructs and figures it out, they're unable to act on their realizations and conclusions. They're unable to act because by the time they figure it out, they're stuck with responsibilities such as a child, a wife, a husband, an image, employment, and a mortgage. The beliefs taught to teenagers and young adults are what eventually cage the woman and man from taking action.

Moreover, social acceptance, and all that comes with and all that doesn't, can motivate a person to accept values that might not be so truthful—no matter the apparent irrationality that clouds them. The truth doesn't seem to matter as much as avoiding the cognitive suffering that comes with social marginalization—in particular, unhappiness.

If change is to come, a generation of people will need to sacrifice popular ideas. If change is to come, a generation must submit to their inherited responsibities.

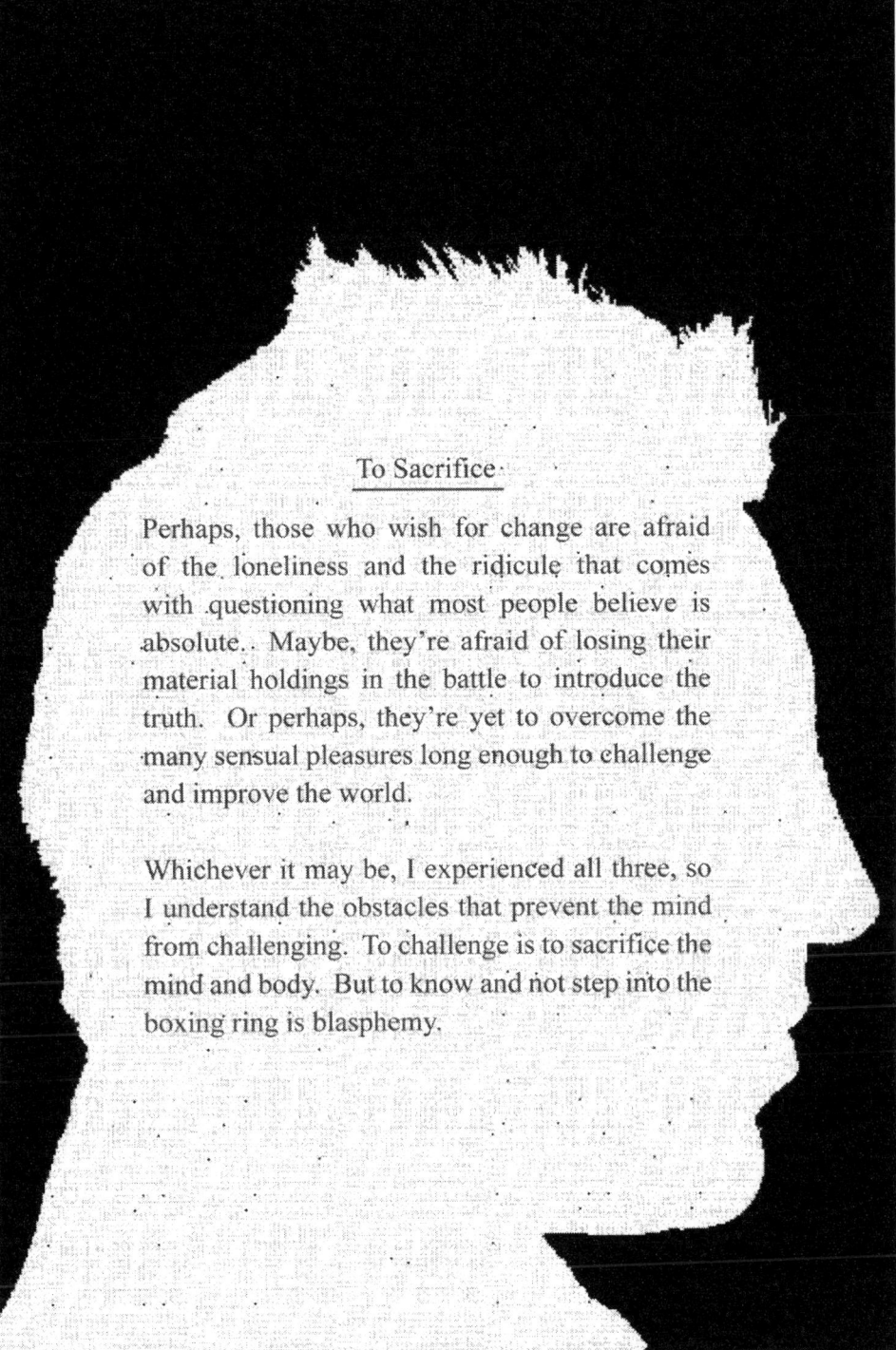

To Sacrifice

Perhaps, those who wish for change are afraid
of the loneliness and the ridicule that comes
with questioning what most people believe is
absolute. Maybe, they're afraid of losing their
material holdings in the battle to introduce the
truth. Or perhaps, they're yet to overcome the
many sensual pleasures long enough to challenge
and improve the world.

Whichever it may be, I experienced all three, so
I understand the obstacles that prevent the mind
from challenging. To challenge is to sacrifice the
mind and body. But to know and not step into the
boxing ring is blasphemy.

CHAPTER 2

CHAMELEON

This chapter will explore popular media's contribution to the theme
of this manuscript.

Tricked

Like a Shakespearean tragedy, tragically, the person is born with little knowledge of what is and what was and the individual is cast into an artificial realm that practices deliberate deception.

Born to high fuel prices, high housing costs, little competition, low wages, a life on credit, the consumer culture, the title of "debt-slave", and on and on, a person will grow assuming that all the mentioned are natural, as the seas or stars, and the suffering attached as a fact of life and unchangeable. Under this impression, few will attempt to eliminate the problems. Under this illusion, people will interpret the short and the thick chains—that prevent the becoming of the ideal human being—as a design of the Universe and her unbreakable principles. Tragically, their conscious awareness and perception of reality will grow within limitations—without them knowing any better.

Tricked are the unborn. Tricked are the unborn and little is done by the living to improve **the built world** they'll grow to experience and to uphold. Little is done because far too many are distracted from recognizing the degenerations—they're caught in the net of a temporary, fleeting, and fake living.

In this reality, one of the principle teachers of the people, popular media, isn't helping a person break free of the distractions. Popular media communicates limited information and doesn't enhance a person's awareness. But this makes sense. To communicate information with the potential to inspire the construction of beliefs that contradict the status quo is counter-productive.

A mind can only create thoughts and make decisions in accordance to the information it houses and the information it doesn't, and the general public are fed information designed to guide their thoughts to intended conclusions. It's a type of mind control and this method was understood and employed long before the Kings of Sumer and by every effective ruler since. So to maintain the power structure, the rulers understand that thoughts must be controlled. In their attempts, so to control the information people will use to formulate their reality, they typically create or infiltrate institutions with the ability to communicate to a large number of people, such as the media. Through them, the rulers teach what they desire the people to know and exclude any knowledge that might threaten their power. And don't think religions and public schools were off-limits, they too were created or infiltrated—some thousands of years ago and some only yesterday. (To learn more about the hijacking of religions, please read *War and Religion*.)

Every generation is born unaware of what is and what was and generations born tomorrow will not know any better if they aren't taught. Is anyone willing to challenge their soon to be Mephistophelian torment? Is there any person strong enough to sacrifice material wishes for tomorrow's children? Here I am, with paper and pen, doing my part. I challenge you to also enter the arena and spar.

....

In this illusion that is living, the status quo has more purpose than the person and an individual's awareness of reality is tampered with to accept the deception. The information given to the people isn't designed to raise enlightened citizens and it's structured to breed servants unaware of their disposition.

Popular media doesn't communicate the knowledge to understand the workings of the world and the division between the rulers and the ruled. I believe this is intentional.

Ancient Tricks

Near the year 1274 B.C., the Egyptian Pharaoh, Ramesses II, was defeated by the Hittites at the Battle of Kadesh. But this isn't what he publicized to his people. Ramesses used the media means of his day and commissioned such things as paintings, sculptures, and wall carvings illustrating him defeating the Hittites.

Ramesses lied to his people to protect his status—a status that depicted him as infallible and above all earthly persons. Although effigies are no longer the predominant tools the ruling class use to communicate a particular view to the general public, the idea is still in play. The only difference is that the television, the radio, the newspaper, the famous, and the journalist are now used to depict what the rulers wish to illustrate.

The goal is the same as it was during Ramesses' reign. Information and misinformation are communicated to enhance and maintain the status of those who regulate, and innumerable lies were given as a truth to achieve this end. Only God knows what is and what isn't a truth.

The popular ideas that govern were seeded to maintain and enhance the status of the ruling class centuries ago. Unaware of their true origins, each person is born innocent to the bigger picture. Moreover, each person is misled to believe in a random and free world that's progressing toward some sort of utopian neighbourhoods. But popular concepts are designed to maintain and enhance the power structure, even though they might be presented in a different form. In this, not only is information limited and presented as complete, sometimes, lies are presented as truth.

The thoughts of the sheep must be controlled. Their wool is what synergizes the infrastructure. Imagine if the individual knew of his or her disposition. How long do you think it would take the people to change their inclinations?

"The greatest enemy of knowledge is not ignorance… it is the illusion of knowledge." — Stephen Hawking

Sometimes, knowledge able to reveal a person's true designation within the manmade world seeps into the common person's sphere of influence. When this occurs, the establishment will typically demonize or ridicule this knowledge. That is, after they create competing notions and controversies to muddy a truth. Under this pretext, born as a simple human, it's so difficult to determine what is and what isn't a truth. Under this pretext, sometimes, it's okay to examine the demonized or ridiculed notions. Sometimes, the truth is where you were told it isn't.

Each person is thrust into the world innocent, and learn each does from a world already in motion. Until a divine intervention or thoughts reach an absolute conclusion, only God knows what is and what isn't.

Weapons of Mass Confusion

The many means available to media, such as radio and television, are the dominant sources from which a person gathers information—outside religions and public education. Moreover, they're the principle sources that shape popular culture.

Yet, if you haven't noticed, occasionally, media does more to misdirect a person's thoughts than it does to enlighten.

The most evident example of the media industry abusing their power is the manner in which they misrepresented Iraq. They reported—without verification—everything the White House said. In the end, the entire world discovered the truth—no weapons of mass destruction in Iraq.

There were no WMDs in Iraq, but the popular media misled their audience and convinced them to think differently. It's as if the masters of media got together and catered a unified message, and simultaneously, struck down any opposing view. Government and corporate propaganda machines were how they behaved.

The reasons for the invasion of Iraq were illegitimate, but the media reported them as legitimate. In doing so, they misled the population to support overseas bloodshed.

We too often assume that popular media communicates information catered by objectivity and truth, and there might have been a time when this was true. But the contemporary scene is home to a mainstream media that doesn't always do what it should, and what you don't know is just as important as what you do.

The media represented a lie as a truth one too many times, and execute they did their own credibility. Not only this, they slowly managed to disease democracy.

Democracy doesn't just involve the majority electing the decision-makers, it's also with a very important prerequisite. The information used to make the decisions and elect must be accurate, complete, relevant, and objective. If it isn't, a person might not make the best democratic decision.

By way of providing selective and misleading information, the popular mediums of communication are, at times, used as propaganda machines by governments and corporations.

There are multiple reasons for this happening and all of them point to money. Big businesses and government, directly and indirectly, control mainstream media through finances and their agendas take the forefront—despite objectivity and truth.

The media industry exists to make money, as such, the media communicates what the money dictates. A corporation or government doesn't necessarily have to own a media outlet, or own shares in an outlet, for it to influence the type of information a media outlet communicates. Corporations and governments spend hundreds of millions in advertising dollars, dollars the media needs to eat. Why would the media slap the hand that feeds?

Popular media occasionally mutates into a misinformation machine. What this means is, the audience is left with little choice but to critically evaluate. It's more than reasonable for the reader, listener, or watcher to employ skepticism and suspicion when reading, listening, or watching.

"To play those millions of minds, to watch them slowly respond to an unseen stimulus, to guide their aspirations without their knowledge—all this whether in high capacities or in humble, is a big and endless game of chess of ever extraordinary excitement." — Sydney West, Founder of the Fabian Society

The Repeaters

After analyzing the type of information the different mediums deliver, it quickly surfaced that the content was centralized and gathered from similar sources. The many different popular mediums were delivering the same messages. Competition between the many outlets was extremely limited. At times, the many different media outlets repeated, word for word, what their supposed competition was communicating. To sample the phenomenon, take a look at the video on the following website. The video is a collage of media clippings from many, many different news outlets showing them communicating, word for word, the same message. (http://www.minds.com/blog/view/100000000000214002/the-best-evidence-you-have-ever-seen-that-puppet-masters-script-mainstream-news-reports).

Due to this lack of competition and originality, it's evident that investigative journalism is a small percentage of the total substance. Albeit, most journalists are trained by their post-secondary education to repeat, and the circumstances of most reporters do not allow them to investigate. Most reporters are not given enough time to put together an investigative piece, and most reporters aren't paid enough to take the time to investigate. They too suffer from the sucky socio-economic waters most people swim in.

Moreover, most journalists gather their information from the same centralized news sources. They gather news not through investigation. Nor do they critically evaluate the hand-me-down information. Because of this centralization, it's not that difficult to spread a lie to an entire nation. To reach a mass audience with a single message, influence the type of information the central sources allow the many reporters to gather.

To that effect, journalists are hazardous when they repeat information without an investigation. Every time they do this, they potentially influence their audience to incorporate inaccurate, incomplete, or misleading information. When they do this, they naturally ambush a person's awareness and all the instruments reliant, such as the notion of democracy.

Perhaps, they're unaware of their role in the war over the minds of the people, and they can be more dangerous than a soulless militant. That is, when they repeat and not investigate.

After analyzing the type of information the different mediums deliver, it quickly surfaced that the content was centralized and gathered from similar sources. The many different popular mediums were delivering the same messages.

....

In America, six companies control all popular media, whereas, a few decades ago, approximately fifty companies owned the different media outlets. The six giants are GE, News-Corp, Disney, Viacom, Time Warner, and CBS. When these big guys collude to design a specific message, there isn't a big enough competitor to mount an effective challenge to their rhetoric.

Kim K and the Band

Among many other things, occasionally, the media is a tool used to distract the general public, and their agents, such as the Kim Kardashians, Miley Cyruses, and the popular girl and boy bands, are made famous to do just that. As are the insignificant trends they're known to set, fads such as twerking.

I write "their agents" because the gatekeepers of media permit the Kim Ks to become popular. The Kim Ks are made popular so to misdirect the human being from intentions with higher meaning and to propagate inconsequential ideas. Why else would the Kim Ks propagate the nonsense they do?

Don't be fooled, very few people become famous without the support of the media's overlords. The popularity of music, musicians, movies, actors, newspapers, reporters, and so on, are not organic—not a sovereign occurence—the masters of media position them as popular, and only a few masters there are. There is a concentration of power within the media industry, and the few who oversee this sector of the market, although they might tell you different, are not interested in a talented person if that talent can not be used to communicate their message. Regrettably, the popular messages they give, too often, do not uplift an individual's state of awareness. If the masters of media were concerned with messages able to enlighten a person, they would create music, movies, newspaper articles, and so on, that enlighten. Instead, the media is occasionally used as a weapon to pacify the public and to teach values that misdirect from a truly higher purpose.

As the past few decades have experienced, the media can attack moral standards. And strangely, the audience too often praises the bullets fired at them. Popular songs, movies, t.v. shows, newspaper articles, and so on are clearly hustling suggestive messages.

Among many other things, occasionally, the media is a tool used to distract the general public, and their agents, such as the Kim Kardashians, Miley Cyruses, and the popular girl and boy bands, are made famous to do just that. As are the insignificant trends they're known to set, fads such as twerking.

....

The illusion is hard to comprehend when our popular culture pretends as if it's natural, and it's difficult to conquer the unhuman happenings when society misinterprets them as a gift from The Celestial.

Cloaked Tentacles

It can no longer be disguised as an expression of art, or a reflection of life, and the media facilitates too much moral corruption for this excuse to fly. It's as if the media strives to encourage the audience to incorporate morally corrupt values.

Without any hesitation, on this point on the thread held from the heavens, the thread of human existence, an age described as the Age of Iron by the ancients, cloaked tentacles routinely tickle the mind's ugly characteristics (**selfish cognitive condition**).

The ancient cultures termed this stage in universal subsistence as the Age of Iron, the epoch considered the era before the Age of Truth. In this era, the forces that nurture the ugly elements of the mind's duality are far more dominant and influential than those that nurture the better members of the cognitive community (**beautiful cognitive condition**).

The forces that nurture the ugly are dominant, and if I'm called to witness, I cannot deny what the ancients scripted. I've battled the tentacles, and in the contemporary world, it feels as if there's no escaping their attempts at activating the mind's lesser such as anger, lust, attachment, **selfish ego**, and greed.

There is no escaping the cloaked tentacles and the corrupt content in movies, TV shows, magazine articles, songs, video games, and online social forums are manifestations of them. Corrupt content is the type which encourages a person to morally compromise or to engage strictly in the senses—information communicated through movies such as Scarface, American Pie, and Fifty Shades of Grey. Television shows such as the Sopranos, Sex in the City, Desperate Housewives, Two and a Half Men,

Jersey Shore, Game of Thrones, The Hills, Temptation Island, Peak Season, and all the soap opera dramas. Music akin to Eazy-E's and Too Short's, and the songs engineered by every other Top 40 performer—they continuously suggest it's okay to morally compromise. The only difference between them and E is that Top 40 artists are subtle with their degenerate messages.

I was born, as you, with little choice but to act vigilant. I was born, as you, with little choice but to tighten the laces, turn the hardhat to the back, assume the position of the thinking man, travel into the mind's value system, and construct a wall to prevent the tentacles from corrupting thoughts and actions. There is no other choice if a person wishes to conquer the darkness.

It can no longer be disguised as an expression of art, or a reflection of life, and the media facilitates too much moral corruption for this excuse to fly. It's as if the media strives to encourage the audience to incorporate morally corrupt values.

....

The term "Age of Iron" refers to the fourth age in a series of four. The ancient cultures of the world such as the Greeks, the Egyptians, the Mayans, and the Indians believed humanity continuously cycles through four ages.

Accordingly, the Age of Iron is the era contemporary humanity is in, and this age is said to be the darkest of all four. The four ages are: The Golden Age of Sat Yuga, the Silver Age of Trayta Yuga, the Brass Age of Dwaapar Yuga, and the Iron Age of Kali Yuga.

The Age of Iron is home to untruths, and to one degree or another, almost all institutions are infected by falsehoods. This includes the culture and the intelligence filled and shaped by those institutions.

Matryoshka

Popular music, movies, and television shows constantly give explicit examples of people in feckless situations and chasing their senses—frolicking, fighting, boozing, or spaced-out on frivolous entertainment. All of which alienate a person from their community, their spirit, the one planet, and benevolent intentions. Disunity and a distracted mind are what popular media appear to instigate amid the masses.

Creature of Compromise

A person's value system, and the associated neural pathways, take the shape of the information most absorbed, repeated, and used. Sadly, elements of modern environments are conditioning and socializing people to, at times, morally compromise.

The human condition has the potential to morally compromise when certain agents of the mind are not influencing thoughts and when certain elements are. The person has the potential when the ugly elements of the mind such as anger, attachment, greed, lust, and/or selfishness are influencing the construction of subconscious and conscious thoughts, and when the benevolent agents of the mind such as empathy, selflessness, truth, and/or compassion are not.

All the compromises a person is capable of such as lying, cheating, stealing, adultery, promiscuity, bullying, injuring another, murder, and exploitation are given potential when the ugly elements are influencing the place thoughts are constructed. When the prospect arises, fiendishly, these elements blur the influence of the munificent agents as smog hides the shine of the stars at night.

The same is true when the benevolent agents are the mind's governors, but in the opposite sense, and they hide the darkness by emanating light. In such a state of mind, a person is at a low risk of moral compromise.

A person's value systems, and the associated neural pathways, take the shape of the information most absorbed, repeated, and used, and modern environments are conditioning and socializing people to, at times, morally compromise. (This idea is further discussed in the fourth chapter, *Self-Sabotage*).

....

A mind that readily compromises moral integrity will naturally ignore collective intention and lean toward a self-centered attitude. This type of awareness rarely recognizes higher intentions and it's incapable of working with other people to achieve a selfless end.

The built world ignores half the person—the human being's spiritual component.

Whom to Blame?

It's easy not to care for the betterment of the world and her people, if a person is not taught to.

The human creature is designed to absorb information and become. Our metaphysical and physical motions are predominantly based on the value system learned and the parts of the mind nurtured. So, whom to blame, the environment or the person?

....

Morality is under attack as it's never been before and entire communities are regressing. No community can truly withstand the peak of anomie. (To further explore how morality is under attack, please read, *Angel vs. Demon*).

The "I" is too big. Each person thinks the world spins for her or him. As if they were the hero or heroine in a film. Advanced societies cannot survive this attitude.

Popular movies and music are the two most influential forces feeding and fattening the "I", and the struggle to live paycheque-to-paycheque contributes to the unhealthy diet and lifestyle.

Skipping Rocks

Last night was a good night. I saw the sun bow, the moon take its place, and the stars slow-dancing on the middle of the lake. Last night was a good night. It allowed my thoughts to travel and enjoy a good conversation at the foot of a lake.

Last night was a good night. Why? Because modern communities prescribe a good conversation as a difficult commodity to come by. Many conversations rarely travel outside the popular culture and the different forms of artificial distractions such as money, sensory pleasure, and misinformation. And when it isn't any of the mentioned, conversations typically entertain what a person has, where a person travelled, what a person saw, how many beers a person drank, the different ways the ego was stroked, another's misfortune, provoked emotions, and the latest of the latest and not about ideas greater than the self.

In these types of conversations, people verbally flex, and mysteriously, they act as if these conversations are required to live like lungs filled with breath.

Perhaps, in their mind's eye they believe the "I" is something more than mortal. Or, it might be that the "I" is unaware of how the "I" becomes. Tell me, why else would the "I" shape its mind to allow for the dissonance, and why else would the "I" verbally strut as if the Master of the Universe, or the Queen of an invisible castle, when most people are in the same boat?

Without prejudice. I must confess. Far too many conversations lack substance and the truth is very much subjective. But I guess this makes sense. The built world conditions beliefs, ideas, wants, expected behaviour, and purposes without pretext. It's difficult to break through the context. I wonder, what would be of us if we were more than human—more than a reflection of the information experienced and absorbed from the world around us? Wait, this isn't the right question. Let me try again. What would be of us if those with the power to teach taught a higher standard of thinking?

Last night was a good night. It was a good night because I participated in a good conversation. I thought about the natural role of a corporation; the responsibility of a government to her children; the attack on our First Mother and her inhabitants; the purpose of nurturing ideas such as truth, love, humility, and compassion; and a people united to achieve a greater end.

Last night was a good night but also unfortunate. Unfortunately, the dead were the only with anything of importance to communicate. Unfortunately, they couldn't elaborate on their written thoughts and interact with my voice to create a new perspective. Imagine that, me and Rousseau skipping rocks by the lake. I wonder if he would be amazed... amazed to see women and men living past their 80s, 50 storey buildings, airplanes, and Escalades? I wonder if he would still be in awe after eaves-dropping on a conversation between a few friends?

The degenerations of modern living are not a mystery. The smoke can be seen in the distance. Unfortunately, the mind has grown insensitive to it and people are pre-occupied with verbally flexing. Thought-bubbles are virtually empty.

Timeout

Every person is moved about like an inanimate object, and every person is tricked to believe the direction taken was a sovereign conclusion and the best decision. So I must ask, in the hope to awaken—Were we really put on this earth to daily give eight-hours of patronage, to have the productions of our blood and labour taken, to live paycheque-to-paycheque, to give forty years toward a mortgage, to sweat for the system when the financial chains will remain regardless, and to thirst strictly for the weekends and retirement? Think about it and ask yourself—Is this true living or the life of a servant?

Sheep are trained to think they're lions—servants are taught to think they're masters. Why else would so many people refuse to recognize their slavish status?

What is good is never easy and only by standing as one can there be real change.

CHAPTER 3
GUBERNATIO

"The power is in the people and politics we address."—Tupac Shakur

Burning Barriers and Cracked Dams

The institutional barriers able to stand in-between private interest and the people, such as unions, to prevent private interest from exploiting the people, are strangely considered by our popular collective intelligence as an evil. In accordance, for over the past few decades, unions, and for that matter, public government, have experienced a drastic reduction in power.

Yet, an entity which represents the people is a good idea. Unless of course, the days of the kings and the queens provided a better living standard. Understand that without institutional barriers to prevent private interest from infringing on the human condition, private interest will infringe on the human condition.

From my observations, the depiction of a union as an evil, and for that matter, a strong and public government, is injected into the popular culture's intelligence as part of a larger program to further reduce the collective strength of a nation's people. The objective is to reduce the influence and power of the people's leadership (their collective representatives).

In the case of a government, a strong and benevolent constitutional entity is capable of reducing the gap that separates the majority of the people from the elite class. Government can do this by providing a rational cost to live, fair wages, competition within the market, better social conditions, a successful means to save cash, and on and on. A strong and benevolent constitutional entity can organize, sustain, and lead an effective campaign against the causes that separate.

From the beginning of this age, the people have struggled against the causes that separate. A struggle each poor and middle-class child inherits, known or not. And from the beginning of this age, the powers that create the causes which reduce the people's living standards have stood a thousand feet tall. Whereas, those brave enough to challenge typically stand a foot or two in comparison. However, a strong government is able to stand toe-to-toe and eye-to-eye. A phenomenon showcased by the Keynesian era. A period in history when the people were finally contenders in the ring of positive social change. Tragically, it wasn't long before the privilege was stripped and the people were pushed back to the days of standing a foot or two in comparison.

The institutional barriers able to represent the needs of the people are depicted as an evil. However, in their truest manifestation, and operated by benevolent and uncorruptable people, such things as unions and governments are a good idea. They're able to improve the living conditions of most people and they're able to prevent private interest from crushing the common woman and man in the search for more capital.

Government is a benefit when government wisely serves the public. However, most politicians have forgotten how to but they've convinced themselves they haven't. They fiddle while we, the Romans, slowly turn to ashes.

Puppets

Constitutional government is the only manufactured entity capable of preventing the regression back to the days of the so-called nobles, and the only manufactured entity capable of protecting, maintaining, and advancing the interests of the people. Nevertheless, government was born without a will and her will is linked to the politicians behind the wheel.

With the appropriate political intention, government can accomplish all reasonable tasks and build a better world. However, without the appropriate political will, constitutional government is just another manufactured entity that restricts the potential of the person and the whole.

In the beginning and in the end, the politicians direct government motion and they can either restrict or unleash government's potential. This said; it seems as if the agents behind the helm didn't use government to protect us, and instead, they used government to facilitate a regression back to the days of the lords, barons, kings, queens, and emperors. The agents behind the helm didn't use government to protect us, and instead, they used government to transform the person into a debt-slave and the debt-slave into a servant—a servant in mind and a servant to the system—a mule for "the movers and the shakers".

The politicians are the will behind the motions of government and the politicians are the gatekeepers of public interest. But tragically, they've forgotten their designation. A consequence of too much wealth in the pockets of a few, puppeteers there are and puppets are one too many political figures.

Luckily for the elected, the people's collective intelligence is still stuck in the Keynesian Era. The majority are yet to validate the notion of puppeteers and puppets. They still believe contemporary politicians are akin to "**Lucius Quinctius Cincinnatus**" with **Cyrus**-like intentions.

The reality is much different, politicians are puppets and the puppeteers are those with large bank balances.

The super-rich control politicians through many methods. The wealthy control through financial contributions, through patronage appointments after leaving politics, by embedding like-minded people amid a political party or in a position to be elected, by spending millions lobbying their agenda, by promising to dump money into the economy, by threatening to pull capital out of the country, and by influencing the creation of policy that empowers them more than government—policies such as the North American Free Trade Agreement. (NAFTA reduces government sovereignty and increases the power of large capital).

Of all the creations sprung from the human mind, democratic and constitutional government is one of the greatest, and although government wasn't created to do as such, government has the ability to build an atmosphere with the potential to allow all people to experience the highest level of living. However, government was born without a will and her will is linked to the politicians behind the wheel.

....

Through public policy, we can journey down a road less traveled. Through public policy, we can remedy the many problems.

To invoke in the common folk a sense of control over their life, this idea of democracy was introduced. Yet, the needs of the common people are readily overlooked and common sense solutions are often dismissed. The true rulers, those behind closed doors, the puppeteers, do as they wish. I guess the purpose of democracy is not to garnish the opinion of the majority, but to make the common folk believe they have a say. Is this a modern occurrence or has it always been like this?

The Pact Between Past People

The artificial world is no longer in the benefit of a person, as it was post World Wars. Government again facilitates a power structure that concentrates worldly resources into the hands of a few. I think it's time to revisit the social contract before it takes something like a World War to destroy the infastructure. It was the destruction of the infastructure, and the displacement of the rulers of this infastructure, that permitted the common person to participate in government, and inevitably, improve the general public's living standard.

It was a golden era. It was the best of times. But the changes made by post World War people are under attack. In many instances, those changes were slowly reversed. For this reason, paycheque-to-paycheque most people live. (For more detail about the regression, take a look at a previous publication, *A Beautiful Destruction*).

Those who lead will tell you one story but the truth can be another.
It's a tactic. Written history is riddled. Evidence she is of the
betrayal. Sleight of hand tricks are used to conceal.

Deliberate Deception

Those who rule sometimes disguise their true intentions. They hide their true reasons and present the public with a false motivation. For example, the American invasion of Iraq was painted as a scheme to free the Iraqis from tyranny. However, it's more than evident that the intentions behind the war were to secure oil, gold, a military foothold, and the American Dollars dominance. Saddam, and others like Gaddafi, were thinking about switching currencies. They were planning to only accept gold for oil and no longer the American Dollar. If this move were made, the devastation of the American Dollar would follow, and inevitably, those dependent on the strength of US currency—the American ruling class.

It's difficult to trust the intention behind the direction politicians occasionally take. The roads they travel, sometimes, are not in the interest of the people but they're presented as if they were. When this is so, the puppets will employ the language of deliberate deception and trick the people into supporting the path they choose. Moreover, they'll package the initiative as the market packages a product—positive words and images will be associated to the project.

NAFTA is an excellent example. It was presented with the latest bells and whistles, and the politicians promised that the agreement would benefit the people. However, the intentions behind NAFTA were to reduce the regulations and the laws that prevent the filthy rich from expanding their influence, wealth, and power. NAFTA has little to do with improving the living standard of the common person. Decades have passed since the ratification of NAFTA and the promises given to the public didn't make an appearance. The nation's GDP increased but the common person economically regressed. The increase went into the pockets of the rich, making them richer, while the "average Joe" went further into debt. (For details to this regression, please read, *A Beautiful Destruction*).

Using a hypothetical example to further illustrate my point, although the model isn't considered hypothetical by some. There's a movement out there suggesting that government will, one day, implant all their citizens with tiny microchips, to better control them. The supposed implants are designed to track a person and release specific chemicals into the body, able to alter an individual's perception and thought process. If this is true, when the rulers present such a plan, they'll attempt to convince the people that the chips are for other reasons than to track them. They'll make claims such as the chip will help the medical industry better serve a person and the true nature of the implant will not be a topic of discussion.

Although the above scenario is quasi-theoretical, a certain happening isn't, and when an initiative isn't in the benefit of the general public, it's packaged as a successful corporation packages a product. Inaccurate associations and titles might also be utilized. I've witnessed this strategy in use and the word "peace" was used to gift wrap "war". The word "prosperity" was used to implement "regressive" economic practices. And the word "freedom" was used to disguise "invasion". In this day and age, a person can't judge a project by its title. The name given by the American Government to the war in Iraq, *Enduring Freedom/Iraqi Freedom*, is a perfect example.

I'm left wondering—How many times have those who rule deceived the people? How much of the world isn't what it's presented as? And can the voting populous truly exercise democracy if the information they're presented with, the information they'll use to make a decision, is incomplete or inaccurate?

In the end, all we can do is critically evaluate what those who rule communicate. Perhaps then, we might not be so easily deceived.

"Language of deliberate deception" is a term referencing the art of presenting inaccurate or incomplete information as if that information is true or complete. If the technique is properly applied, a person will believe he or she independently reached the intended justification or conclusion.

"There will be in the next generation or so a pharmacological method of making people love their servitude and producing dictatorship without tears, so to speak, producing a kind of painless concentration camp for entire societies so that people will in fact have their liberties taken away from them but will rather enjoy it." — Aldous Huxley (1894- 1963)

The Divine Right of Kings

The divine right of kings is a thing of the past and there was a time when rulers were harmonized with heaven.

Long ago, as recorded by the ancient Indian thinkers, when the alignment of the visible planets was not as today, in an era designated as Sat Yug (the Age of Truth), kings were heavenly in their rule.

The rulers of then were kept in check by their awareness of a greater reality, and benevolence, compassion, truth, honour, and virtue were the clays that moulded their rule and legacy. But that was then and the contemporary kings no longer behave as such. Perhaps, it's the doing of Kali Yug (the Age of Darkness)? Perhaps, it's a disease and the contemporary rulers are infected? To be honest, only The Great Architect knows the cause and I can only pretend.

Nevertheless, a deduction there is, the contemporary kings and queens are far from divine. If their motivations and behaviour were aligned to heaven, the world would not be plagued by war, slavery, hunger, poverty, pollution, and environmental destruction.

The rulers of the world can improve the conditions of the planet and her people, but how to convince them to behave as their ancient predecessors?

"Since I entered politics, I have chiefly had men's views confided to me privately. Some of the biggest men in the U.S., in the field of commerce and manufacturing, are afraid of somebody, are afraid of something. They know that there is a power somewhere so organized, so subtle, so watchful, so interlocked, so complete, so pervasive, that they had better not speak above their breath when they speak in condemnation of it." — American President, Woodrow Wilson

Donald Trump

A large minority of people are awake to the corrupt nature of the contemporary eco-political arrangement. Donald Trump's anti-establishment rhetoric managed to herd them. Simultaneously, it gave the disenchanted hope and kept them non-violent. Unfortunately, "the Don" has too much to lose and he will not truly challenge the establishment. Those who challenge are typically vilified through the media and then shot or poisoned, and their families marginalized. "The Don" knows this.

Yet, the media does actively vilify Donald, and in this scenario, I'm inclined to think this too is scripted.

The anti-establishment message is all a show and it wouldn't surprise me to find out that "the Don" and "the establishment" orchestrated it together.

Publicly, the establishment has distanced itself from Donald Trump, but what happens in public and what happens behind closed doors can be two different realities.

The power structure is aware that many millions of people are frustrated and angry with the system. Trump and his anti-establishment message is just a means to pacify the people until the next election.

Those who rule are much smarter than the public. A few steps ahead of the ruled they stand. Will this situation ever change? I don't know. The last time it did, it took a worldwide deluge.

....

The Trump Show not only pacifies, it also distracts. So, we must ask— What are the overlords busy with, and how much thicker will the chains be after they're done?

Party Loyalty

Political parties and party loyalties divide. Trump's presidential campaign and victory, and before his, Obama's, brought this to light as no other in modern times. Each political side is more concerned with insulting every aspect of the other party's leader, members, and platform, instead of honestly discussing the issues.

Party loyalties prevent each side from recognizing the good in the other, and each side employs bully tactics to deflect attention away from their opponent's progressive ideas. Moreover, many haven't read their party's platform, or their opponent's, and their political knowledge is gathered from Facebook memes, through conversations with other politically illiterate loyalists, and party pamphlets. Maybe, that's why they constantly flip-flop on the issues. Maybe, that's why they rarely present solutions that tackle the roots of a problem. Perhaps, that's why they bully those who disagree. Knowledgeable people debate ideas and rarely resort to calling the opponent degrading names.

Clear divisions there are amid the people. The political process is capable of bettering the living standards of an individual, but party loyalties pit the sheep against each other. The voters should be aligning with progressive ideas and not political brackets, but individual ambitions and the sense of belonging to a gang too often override the ability to reason.

In lieu of, when those disenchanted with the eco-social setup do muster the motivation to invoke the political process, in hopes of alleviating their hardships, party loyalties and party rhetoric further alienate their aspirations.

The contemporary political process is too confrontational and bullying is now acceptable. The ancient Romans too suffered under similar divisive circumstances, just before the fall of their empire. They lost it all and we could too if truth, respect, honour, and ethics isn't reintroduced.

Political parties and party loyalties divide. Trump's presidential campaign and victory, and before his, Obama's, brought this to light as no other in modern times. Each political side is more concerned with insulting every aspect of the other party's leader, members, and platform, instead of honestly discussing the issues.

....

Many party loyalists are so because they hope to one-day garnish party favour. Perhaps, they're looking for a job or hoping the party selects him or her to run in a future election. And the party executives are fully aware of a loyalist's ambitions. They dangle the prospects like a carrot on a stick, and for that carrot, if they could, some loyalists would sell their first born and prostitute their soul.

The needs of the people sometimes call for free market principles to reign, and sometimes they call for a Keynesian approach. In this, the voter must be flexible and willing to change political sides—allying with those with the best plan to meet present needs. To be stringent with a vote isn't in the best interest of the voter. Nothing but a mule one becomes, chasing a carrot.

Yesterday is Today

I'm reclined back and listening to the bass from the drum. Inside my mind, cognitive agents are wrangling together words to express my thoughts. What metaphor, which font, and how to express myself without pointing fingers at the present? Perhaps, I should look to the past to illustrate my latest revelation, because only the faces have changed and not the illusion.

The European Monarchs of old didn't really battle each other, and if one monarchy fell, by way of the general public, the other monarchs would descend on that territory to restore the fallen family's power. The story of Napoleon Bonaparte illustrates this fact well. Napoleon freed his people from the French Monarchy to only have the other European Monarchs, turn by turn, attack him. They eventually defeated Napoleon and restored monarchal power. They then tampered with the history books to depict him as a troublemaker.

The ruling families of yesterday belonged to the same circle, and more often than not, to the same bloodline, and each had a territory they governed. Sometimes, like siblings, they quarrelled. Sometimes, like drunken friends, they wrestled. And sometimes, like spiteful ex-lovers, they warred. But in the end, they always made-up and resumed their control over the world. The same is true of the modern world and only the faces have changed and not the illusion.

....

Occasionally, even in this era, a heavenly king will rise. The last known celestial leader to embrace this age is Guru Gobind Singh. His accomplishments are yet to be measured. For example, in December, 1704, he and 40 of his followers battled one-million Mughal soldiers, led by Wazir Khan. Guru Gobind walked away from the battlefield unharmed. Only a person touched by The Great Architect can do this. He writes of his victory in a letter to the Mughal Emperor, titled, *Zafarnama*. Sadly, all his followers perished in the fight, including two of his sons.

Ten-thousand tales there are of Gobind's greatness. Where to begin and where to end? If you're into the study of great personalities, he might be someone of interest. If you'd like to learn more about one of his greatest achievements, the Khalsa, please read, *Confessions: a lion's roar--a poet's war*.

"For we are opposed around the world by a monolithic and ruthless conspiracy that relies on covert means for expanding its sphere of influence—on infiltration instead of invasion, on subversion instead of elections, on intimidation instead of free choice, on guerrillas by night instead of armies by day. It is a system which has conscripted vast human and material resources into the building of a tightly knit, highly efficient machine that combines military, diplomatic, intelligence, economic, scientific and political operations.

Its preparations are concealed, not published. Its mistakes are buried not headlined. Its dissenters are silenced, not praised. No expenditure is questioned, no rumor is printed, no secret is revealed." — American President, John F. Kennedy

Platonopolis

It is vital to understand the history of civilizations so to understand the history in the making, and the utopian city of Platonopolis contains a very important lesson.

In the mid-second century, Plotinus conceptualized a city he called "Platonopolis". A student of Neoplatonism, Plotinus desired to build a city echoing Plato's philosophy. Envisioned as a place to enlighten the Roman public and to help a person reach a higher standard of living—in mind, body, soul, and material, Platonopolis was rejected by the Roman ruling class.

The rulers of the day dismissed the idea. They did so because an environment able to empower a common person isn't in their benefit. An enlightened populous isn't so easy to exploit.

For the same reason, throughout history, great storehouses of knowledge akin to the Library of Alexandria, the magnificent Library of Nalanda, the Mayan libraries of the Yucatan, the Library of al-Hakam II, the Xianyang Palace Library, and the Sikh Reference Library were destroyed. Along with libraries, the people who taught any knowledge, philosophy, or history able to inspire a people were also hunted and hung. Hunting those who awaken others is still a thing, and defamation seems to be the modern means at eliminating them.

The exploitation of the masses is what empowers the ruling classes and if the people realize their standing as servants, who live in darkness, the ruling elite will eventually lose their status. But so long as the exploited members of society can not conceptualize their disposition, they can not challenge those who exploit them. For this reason, knowledge was and is limited, and the popular knowledge serves only to train a good servant. It's an old tactic and most successful rulers use it.

Take the story of Platonopolis as you will, and even though modern communities are filled with technologies the Roman people were never with, contemporary cities are no Platonopolis. The rulers still resist the creation of such an environment.

Those who desire social change typically gravitate to conventional groups, means, methods, and theories. But none are identifying the root of the problem, and thus, true change is never truly obtained.

For this, some groups, means, methods, and theories were established. Their design is to waste the time and energy of an individual who desires social change.

No Society Wants You to Become Wise

The following is a transcription of approximately the first four minutes to the lecture, *"No Society Wants You to Become Wise"*, by Osho.

"No society wants you to become wise. It is against the investment of all societies. If people are wise, they cannot be exploited. If they are intelligent, they cannot be subjugated; they cannot be forced in a mechanical life, to live like robots. They will assert, they will assert their individuality. They will have the fragrance of rebellion around them. They would like to live in freedom. Freedom comes with wisdom, intrinsically—they are inseparable. And no society wants people to be free. The communist society, the fascist society, the capitalist society, the Hindu, the Mohammaden, the Christian, no society... would like people to use their own intelligence, because the moment they start using their own intelligence, they become dangerous. Dangerous to the establishment; dangerous to the people who are in power; dangerous to the 'haves'; dangerous to all kinds of oppression, exploitation, suppression; dangerous to the churches; dangerous to the states; dangerous to the nations. In fact, a wise man is a fire, alive, a flame. He would like rather to die than to be enslaved. Death will not matter him much, but he cannot sell his life to all kinds of stupidities, to all kinds of stupid people. He cannot serve them. Hence the societies, down the ages, have been supplying you with false knowing. That's the very function of your schools, colleges, universities. They don't serve you, remember, they serve the past, they serve the vested interest. Of course, they go on puffing your ego bigger and bigger. They go on giving you more and more

degrees. Your name becomes longer and longer, but just the name, you go on becoming shorter and shorter. A point comes there are only certificates and the man has disappeared. First, the man carries the certificates, then the certificates carry the man. The man is long dead."

"No Society Wants You To Become Wise". Youtube. Original Date Unknown. Internet. September 19, 2015. Transcript. [https://www.youtube.com/watch?v=Kll1XQ90JOs]

His Story

European style history suggests that the human lived in a cave not too long ago. It further implies that contemporary societies, with all their flaws, are far superior to those of the distant past. But according to the older cultures of the world such as the Indians, Chinese, Mayans, Sumerians, and Egyptians, modern civilizations are not the first to exhibit advanced technology or an advanced understanding of nature. The ancient Indians and Chinese are said to possess flying machines. The Sumerians mapped the planets in our solar system thousands of years before modern astronomy did. The Egyptians were building wonders as the Sphinx ten-thousand years in the past. And the Mayans were able to calendar thousands of years into the future.

The ancient world wasn't as primitive as some might suggest, and their history of civilizations, as told by, for example, the Indians and noted in the Vedic literature, stretches back millions of years. This said, civilizations are constantly destroyed and humanity experiences brief periods in which the people live as the cave paintings suggest. Many times this has happened. Many times civilizations were reset. The European style history only begins some time after the last civilization destroying cataclysm.

The history of the world is much more complex and advanced than suggested by mainstream historians and archaeologists. The reason mainstream academics deny the past is to give the impression that the structure of modern society is the cream of the crop, and the dominant beliefs of contemporary society are also. If it's revealed that ancient cultures weren't as backward as they're depicted as, people might also give more credence to their belief systems. The ancient belief systems are completely opposite to modern values and they focus more on a spiritual existence than a material living. If the modern belief systems were to fall, so would those who benefit from their dominance. Thus, the people are kept in the dark and their true beginnings and potential are stored behind hidden vaults. It sounds like a conspiracy but it's not. The evidence to support the notion of ancient advanced civilizations is there and researchers such as Graham Hancock and Micheal Cremo are two of many who've done the homework. Take a read through their books if you'd like to know where I'm coming from. I discuss some of their findings in my upcoming publications.

European style history suggests that the human lived in a cave not too long ago. It further implies that contemporary societies, with all their flaws, are far superior to those of the distant past. But according to the older cultures of the world such as the Indians, Chinese, Mayans, Sumerians, and Egyptians, modern civilizations are not the first to exhibit advanced technology or an advanced understanding of nature.

The built world has the potential to benefit all people. The design isn't all that flawed. Only the selfish and greedy ideologies driving it are corrupt.

A Flower in February

The hands of time and circumstance temporarily made peace. In the process, they shook hands and gave birth to a continent with the potential to be.

Why they finally came together is a mystery. Who knows? Perhaps, it's a natural occurrence as the changing of seasons, a natural evolution. Or perhaps, it's a fluke as life is to a scientist. Whatever the reason, one thing is certain, and that certainty is the New World's potential to be, to be an example.

An example of the next stage in humanity's evolution—removed from war, poverty, illiteracy, and the degenerations of our contemporary history—designed by peaceful, truthful, respectful, resourceful, and enlightened surroundings. These are the conditions required for the human creation to bloom and be.

To bloom, to bloom and be... Perhaps, as a summer flower in February, the New World is yet to bloom and be. To be... to be like Gobind's **Warrior-Poet** or Plato's Philosopher-King.

The New World is destined for greatness. Providence. F. Bacon's new Atlantis. This backwardness is simply the Old grasping at the power it once held. The attempt is futile. Fate is the gardener. The New will bloom, become, and fragrance the world.

....

If you'd like to know more about Gobind's Warrior-Poet, please read, *Confessions: a lion's roar—a poet's war.*

Newish World

Since we're close to the subject, I guess I'll share with you a secret. The New World isn't all that new and many cultures from around the world, before Colombus, set foot on American soil. The Indians (from India), the Greeks, the Egyptians, the Romans, the Vikings, the Chinese, and the Africans are some of these cultures. The reason you might not know of their American connection is because the history books, written by the victors, fail to mention it.

Interestingly, the Greeks write that they visited hundreds of years before the birth of Jesus. The Greeks viewed the "New World" as a Godly paradise, and instead of exploiting it, with respect to "The All-Mind" within all minds, they left the land to her own devices. Supposedly, the ancient cultures possessed detailed and accurate world maps. The Pieri Reese Map, the Merkator Map, and the Arontios Phenious Map are said to be copies of those ancient maps. On these maps, there is no ice covering Antarctica and the topography is accurately recorded.

Some people believe that the ancient cultures of the world were isolated from each other, but that's not what the different ancient cultures suggest. Oceans were highways and not barriers dividing them. The ancients were advanced people and more than capable of building large ships. Evidence of their building mechanics can still be found all over the world—the Pyramid of Giza (Egypt), Gobekli Tepe (Turkey), Ggantija (Maltese island of Gozo), Yonaguni Monument (Japan), Sacsahuaman (Peru), and Pumapunku (Bolivia). Modern minds still do not completely understand how several of these structures were constructed, or what type of technology was used to do so.

CHAPTER 4

SELF-SABOTAGE

The greatest obstacles hindering a better world and a higher living standard are those who would benefit. The greatest enemies are the enemies within.

When you ask, *"Where has hope gone?"* And I answer, *"Living with Egyptian gods"*. I imply that unity is dead and it lives amid giants, dragons, and leprechauns.

Comatose

The cost to live has touched the sky, the masses wait under the table for the crumbs from the pie, and self-interest and voracity occupy while the youth in us dies. But it's as if the world tickled the collective **claustrum** and rendered everybody unconscious to the backwardness and the lies.

The artificial coupling between greed and the human being is destroying. The evidence is such that the power of the sun would be the appropriate metaphoric expression to describe it. Undeniable the proof is. Yet, most people do little to peacefully defy and defend.

In addition to the explanations provided in the previous chapters, another reason little is done is because the people are trained to harbour a conflictual attitude toward each other. Such an attitude obstructs the mind from greater meaning and purpose, and such a cognitive creature doesn't work well with others—it prevents people from banding together to achieve a common end.

This chapter will explore the ideas of moral compromise and conflict—the dissonance they emanate, the self-inflicted suffering they result in, and their ability to create islands from a single landmass.

Controlled Conflict and Disunity

To maintain and to predict, the system needs a compliant labour pool in disunity and conflict.

A labour pool in disunity and conflict is required to occupy the mind during the downtime, and to keep the mind compliant to given beliefs, wants, and built designs.

For the system to maintain and to grow, the labour pool must be dependent on it as a welfare recipient. For this reason, the general public are given just enough so not to resist. For this reason, long term security is constantly under threat. For this reason, a mortgaged life exists. For this reason, a paycheque provides only two weeks of breath. And for this reason, the general public are encouraged to consume without reason.

Appreciate that the minds of the majority must be kept submissive to the overall system for the system to maintain and to grow. Not only that, the minds of the majority must also be kept in a state of disunity and conflict. A peaceful mind might realize the people's status. If the general public recognize their substandard disposition, and if the people are able to work together, they might unite and change their place on the **Western Caste system**.

The people are kept in a state of controlled conflict in many ways and all of them are designed to trigger a person's hate. The labelling, lying, gossiping, bullying, and marginalizing are manifestations of.

To maintain and to predict, the system requires a compliant labour pool in disunity and conflict. That is, if the contemporary kings of the machine wish to have more to have. A mind rested, educated, peaceful, and free to think freely might realize and act as an enemy. A labour pool in harmony might adjust the given value system and demand a better living. Dangerous this is for the contemporary elite and their god, "greed".

The system is a series of constructs designed to guide the movement of us and resources. And when not that, the system keeps the proletarians disunited, stressed, and in conflict. Divide, conquer, and control are the objectives.

Self-Inflicted

The mind is readily distracted by forces outside the human condition and by way of many methods such as controlled conflict. But did you know... outside forces are not the most potent. Self-distraction is.

Self-distraction is a common thing and the person too often distracts their own mind from intentions with higher meaning. This is so because many, many people have a difficult go at being alone with their thoughts. They find it easier and less painful to distract the mind when arises a moment of inactivity or cognitive silence.

In this self-inflicted injury, the misuse of technology, such as a Smartphone, contribute heavily. Consider them like an enabler to a junkie, or energy to a disease.

Anomie

Is it just me or is popular culture courting anomie? Can it be that the effort is made so to alienate a person's **Thought Energy** (time and space of thought) from a higher intelligence?

What is a higher intelligence?

A higher intelligence refers to a set of beliefs manifest through behaviour:

•Beliefs that curb selfish desires and behaviour, immoral desires and behaviour, non-virtuous desires and behaviour.

•Beliefs that encourage emotional stability, rationality, humility, spirituality, compassion, empathy, love, etc.

•Beliefs that instil a want for self-actualization, a collective purpose, knowledge, truth for the sake of truth, virtue for the sake of virtue, honour for the sake of honour, etc.

Popular culture has the power to influence beliefs. This is no secret. And if enough people are persuaded of a particular value, the people will self-perpetuate it. It's a vicious cycle. But why would the forces that be attack a higher intelligence and trigger a state of anomie?

Anomie references a state of being devote of a higher intelligence and anomie naturally thwarts unity. People who lack a higher intelligence are with a greater potential to compromise morals. This type of person has a difficult go at working with other people to achieve a common goal. They're also typically the first to sellout a movement. That is, if they even bother to contemplate the status quo. The fact of the matter is, those willing to morally compromise are the least likely to question—so long as the means to their moral compromise and their material desires are satisfied.

Is it just me or is popular culture courting anomie? Can it be that the effort is made so to alienate a person's Thought Energy (time and space of thought) from a higher intelligence?

....

Moral compromise weakens the magnetic field a person emanates. When the field is fragile, the person is easily suggestible. This idea is further explained in the book, *Angel vs. Demon*.

Half a man and half a woman. Our popular culture and our collective intelligence have seduced "the me" to live as an island. Disconnected we are from our fellow humans.

Mike Bhangu

Uncle Toms

A morally strong value system is constantly attacked. This disrupts a united front, a sense of personal sacrifice, and higher intention. The assault appears to intensify toward the more oppressed groups within the caste of the ruled, such as the African-Americans and the women.

In both cases, soon after gaining recognition as equal to "the white man", the moral standards of these two groups were challenged. Morality was and is attacked through the popular media and the trends they set such as twerking and the gangster attitude.

Morality is attacked   because a group of people who lack a higher intelligence, or in other words, are morally corrupt, can not work together to achieve a higher and benevolent purpose.   The temperaments of immorality naturally block the notion of unity and the many personal sacrifices required to bring forth positive change.   Moreover, a morally corrupt person doesn't value a higher life purpose, or working to improve the general good.   Their mindset prefers to please primarily the self and selfish desires, and this state of mind doesn't perceive any personal gain by giving time, resources, and energy to improving society or the general public's living standard.

....

Feminism is almost dead and top-down fades such as twerking hospitalized the movement.

The Nature of the Human

Years were spent gazing at the night canvas so to connect the shiny specks of dust. On an unknown number of occasions the sun bowed and the moon took its place—changes occurred beneath my feet—the grass grew above my waist. And almost every changing of guard brought with it notions unaligned to those built inside the popular crate—such as the idea that revealed the nature of the human being.

Unfortunately, the revelation was a little depressing. Why? Well, when man mastered the ability to instil beliefs and wants within a person's value system, he inadvertently or purposely stole the greatest responsibility.

You see, if born amongst diamonds a person will translate and shine. If born orbiting a person will translate and rise. If born in the air a person will translate and fly. But born to the artificial hardships of the 21st century and the upside-down popular beliefs, a person is simply passing time before they die.

The temperament of the human creature is to become and to befall the environments around him or her. This is a truth no woman or man can outrun, and those who rule understand the person's natural disposition.

"Public schools are the nurseries of all vice and immorality."
— Henry Fielding

Deficient is Public Education

The human condition suffers because the system is unaware of the human potential, and the public education system is deficient and can be 100 fold better.

You see, the system underestimates the person and under-educates him and her. Not knowing or not caring, the system nurtures an unfilled potential.

So please, someone tell the decision-makers that the students have the ability to learn much more. Teach the high school senior students university equivalent liberal arts information (sociology, philosophy, political science, etc.) and experience a much more enlightened people. Eventually, public schools will become more than daycare centers, and eventually, the system will create better people.

The schooling system is capable of producing so much more than what it already has. However, missing is a challenge and a good education. Moreover, little is done to counter the negative values so readily communicated by elements of popular culture.

Perhaps, a good education is missing because the ideologies that drive the system of production, distribution, and consumption do not need a highly educated population to function and to grow. If the sheep were truly educated, who will want to or have a need to do the hard labour required by the system? And who will consume without reason?

A few more questions for the readers still reading. Will there be anyone blind enough to soldier? Will there be anyone left to subject the mind, body, and soul to a nine-to-five for little gain? Will there be anyone willing to mortgage three-quarters of their life? Will there be anyone selfish enough to breed screws for the system? And will there be anyone left in a state of anomie and controlled conflict?

The human condition suffers because the system is unaware of the human potential, and the public education system is deficient and can be 100 fold better.

> *"What sculpture is to a block of marble, education is to the human soul."* — Joseph Addison

....

Caged are young men by public education. What is taught over 12 years can be learned in 4. Trapped are the young and the strong because this demographical is historically the arms of a revolution.

To make matters worse, in the cage, men are taught to further trap the self after they exit. Indoctrinated they are to marry, have children, nine-to-five it, and on and on. All of which prevent the fighter from fighting for true change.

Built to Become

I was built like this, a chameleon in essence, and I naturally become my environments. To that extent, to be or not to be? Wait, let me rephrase. What be the thing I'm bred to be?

King of the Castle Complex

The past several decades have seen the emergence of an undiagnosed disease. It's a disease that's infected every other human being. The disease I speak of is "the King of the Castle Complex".

Common symptoms of the disease are an inability to accept positive criticism, to accept advice, to accept rejection, to accept another's greatness, to accept that one might be mistaken, and to accept that another might be accurate. In a nutshell, it's difficult for a person who suffers from the complex to perceive the self as less or as a subordinate. They prefer to think they're perfect diamonds who live amid diamonds in the rough. Unfortunately, when this perfection is threatened, they lash out.

They can lash out in many different ways. All of which are negative and attempts to lessen the value of the person who threatened, and to regain the personal loss of value felt. For example, a threatened individual might respond by attributing degrading and demeaning words to the one who presented the challenge. Slander is a choice weapon used by the likes of them.

Sometimes, it doesn't even take a threat. Those infected by the disease too often speak negatively about other human beings. Moreover, they'll keep the past alive for as long as they can—they don't allow other people to live down past mistakes. For example, a person might've lapsed in judgement a decade ago but they'll label according to that lapse. That person might've invented a medicine akin to penicillin but they'll still be remembered, by the infected, according to the mistakes of their past.

It's as if those infected live in the negative, and it's as if they do not realize that we're all human—imperfect and capable of mistakes. But just as capable is our potential to improve, just as capable is our potential to make good, and just as capable is our potential to grow a halo.

I want to use the word "primitive" but this word conjures too many negative connotations. However, there is no other word I can think of that so fully describes the blood that pumps through the phenomenon.

The past several decades have seen the emergence of an undiagnosed disease, the King of the Castle Complex, and it's a byproduct of the information our popular culture delivers. Not surprisingly, the disease contributes to the lack of unity. It's near-impossible for those who suffer from the complex to collude and achieve a benevolent and selfless end. Is this why the disease is yet to be addressed?

....

The King of the Castle Complex is typically accompanied with another ailment—an unwillingness to critically evaluate. Instead, based on limited information, assumptions are made and conclusions are drawn. To further the damage, the assumptions and conclusions might lead to actions. It's a cycle of ignorance.

Not much can be accomplished when too many kings and queens there be and no soldiers in the army.

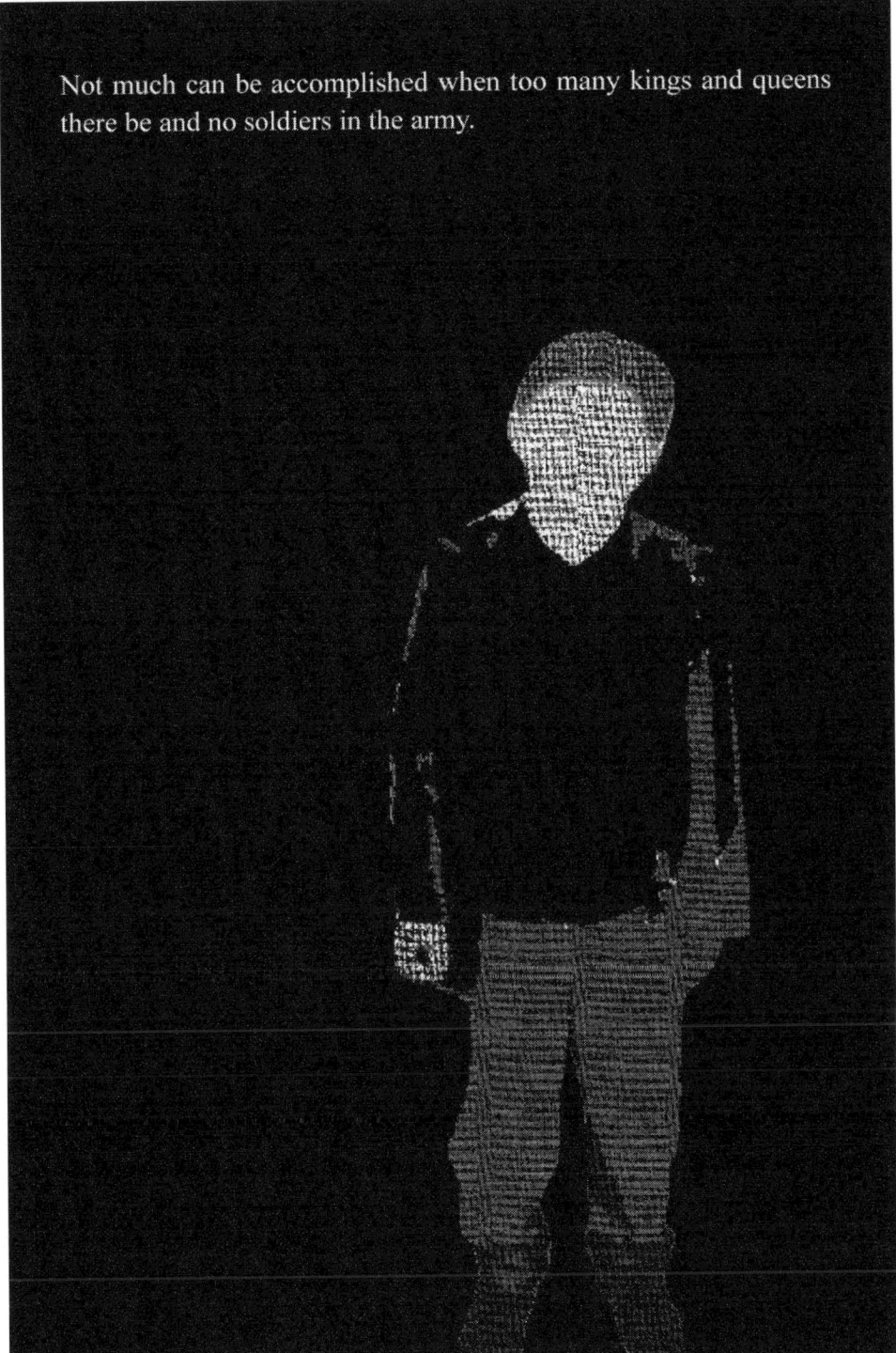

The Rise of the Caveman

The rise of the caveman isn't indefinite or something from a science fiction flick. The happening is an observable fact within developed nations, and a black-eye they give to communities progressing towards a higher living.

The term "caveman" is one used to describe the person who struts, talks, and thinks of the self as **Gordon Gekko**, the godfather, or the king of a castle. The definition also includes all the thugs, the players, the bullies, the crooked CEOs, the warring politicians, the corrupt cops, the crack-dealers, and the gangsters. All of the mentioned are caveman, and this because of their perspective of the self and the world around them.

The caveman's outlook is extremely narrow and a person-turned-caveman dedicates little thought to the consciousness of others. The caveman does whatever he wants, regardless if the behaviour transferred suffering to another or life in general. In light of the caveman's own wants, all else is acceptable collateral damage.

The rise of the caveman isn't indefinite or something from a science fiction flick, and there appear to be enough people in this category that a new culture has emerged.

A new culture has materialized and it's a culture with no loyalty to any of the pre-consumer cultures, and it actually stems through the culture of the consumer. The Chinese, the Africans, the Europeans, the Indigenous, and on and on, they're all subject to the culture of the caveman

.

All cultures are subject to the culture of the caveman so long as all are dominantly taught by the culture of the consumer.

The emergence of the caveman appears to hold a relationship with the type of information popular Western culture communicates, and the type of information it's evolved to dismiss as irrelevant. Typically, when a new element within a culture emerges or when a new culture emerges, there's first a change in the information popular culture and the collective intelligence communicate and do not communicate.

The most susceptible to a change in the information available are the have-nots and this includes the contemporary middle-class person. They're most susceptible because they can't change the structure of the built environment so to shape it and the information it delivers, and they do not have the resources to remove the self from the equation.

To remove the self from a contaminated environment is the ideal option when attempting to protect the mind from corrupt information. Think of it like this. When the Plague that devastated Europe hit, of the haves and the have-nots, the have-nots suffered more per capita. They were unable to leave the crowded cities and villages, whereas, the haves were able to remove themselves from the sullied surroundings.

The haves are with a greater chance at surviving but this doesn't imply that the have-nots can't endure the contamination. Those sub-cultures or groups that preach and practice a higher value system have a strong chance of surviving the encounter. Notwithstanding the fact that what we consider a sub-culture was once a dominant culture somewhere in the world, and several of the dominant cultures of the planet were attacked not too long ago.

The cultures of the world were besieged by the tyranny of colonial powers, and although the colonialists purposely corrupted the cultures they contacted, hope there is for those who retained their cultural foundations.

But those who lost this link are more susceptible to the culture of the caveman.

The colonialists purposely infected the higher intelligence of the cultures they came into contact with. Without a link to a higher intelligence as a shield to defend against, a caveman can rise from within a woman or man, and a caveman is easier to defeat and control than a person with a higher intelligence. It's as simple as that.

Like a demonic possession, the caveman can rise and take hold of a woman or man, and the emergence seems to hold a relationship with the type of information popular culture communicates, and the type of information it's evolved to dismiss. Popular environments have morphed to reduce the amount of virtuous and benevolent information they communicate— information that nurtures the collective agents of the mind like empathy, truthfulness, selflessness, humility, and compassion.

The decline in this type of information is, in part, due to the decline in religion. For the most part, religion does inspire ideas able to keep the ugly half of the mind's duality at bay, and religion does encourage a person to function through the beautiful half of the mind. However, religion went in decline because it lied one too many times. As religion declined, the other elements of society didn't rise to fill the void.

The term "caveman" is one used to describe the person who struts, talks, and thinks of the self as Gordon Gekko, the godfather, or the king of a castle. The definition also includes all the thugs, the players, the bullies, the crooked CEOs, the warring politicians, the corrupt cops, the crack-dealers, and the gangsters. All of the mentioned are caveman, and this because of their perspective of the self and the world around them.

Caveman-Like

They worship the material as the ancient Greek poets worshipped Apollo—mesmerized they are by its demi-god like power.

They believe in violence without the knowledge in the art of—violence is always the last resort.

They cultivate insecurities, fabrications, and dissonance—most react to the slightest perception of a pride challenged.

They compromise honour, virtue, and dharma (righteousness) come selfish ends—someone forgot to teach the rules of a Karmatic existence.

They love the "I" more than the collective—public good is a fairytale like that of Merlin.

....

To further explore the cultural elements that nurture the caveman, please read, *Angel vs. Demon.*

Misplaced Hate

I wonder... How many were mislabelled and discredited? How many conformed to the ideas they challenged? How many were wrongly shackled and imprisoned? And how many advancements did the human race miss?

I ask the above because the masses have a bad habit of hating ideas and people they don't understand. In particular, the socially conscious rebel and their notions, even though the socially conscious rebel is responsible for the social, spiritual, political, and economic progress the people have made since the beginning of this age. Without them, we might still be serfs in a type of technologically advanced middle-age feudal cage.

I'm not sure why this phenomenon exists. I don't know why so many hate the people able to envision a better existence. But what is certain is that the hate can pull, dull, mislabel, discredit, shackle, and/or assimilate a rebel and the substance that bestowed the name. We seem to police each other but not in a constructive way.

Oddly enough, most people in the maze have, at one point or another, adopted the mentality of a socially conscious rebel. Most people can relate to the thoughts a rebel's mentality produces and the illusion those thoughts are able to implode. However, most people can't handle the suffering attached to the title and they silently take their place in the maze. This said; some conformed for justifiable reasons. Perhaps, they fell in love. Perhaps, they mothered or fathered a child. Or maybe, they made a million.

Most of the time it's none of the above and the socially conscious rebel surrenders the title so to appease the people around her or him. Again, even this is a justifiable reason. It's very difficult to fit in or to satisfy the innate need for belonging when you walk, talk, and think a little differently. Sometimes, the differences can provoke others to hate and the hate can crush the insides of a person.

Whatever the reason is, it's as if the masses pull the rebel back in, and I can't help but wonder what might've been if the rebels were left to their mechanisms.

Perhaps, there wouldn't be poverty. Perhaps, there wouldn't be manmade divisions dividing the holy. Perhaps, democracy would actually be. Perhaps, our First Mother (planet earth) would be strong and healthy. Perhaps, we'd live for more than two weeks. Perhaps, the term debt-slave wouldn't breathe. And maybe, people would love before they hate.

In the beginning and in the end, it's the many forms of hate people are capable of delivering that more so hinder the progression of a nation's people. The hate prevents the masses from uniting under one banner. Without unity, the public can't take the actions required to break the invisible chains that every single mouse endures. Without unity, the world will be no better.

....

The sheep point at each other as the problem and not the shepherds and sheepdogs that divide them. Tactfully divided, perpetually distracted, and stuck in a cycle of hating each other until the transition to the Age of the Water Bearer.

"Marco Polo describes a bridge, stone by stone. 'But which is the stone that supports the bridge?' Kublai Khan asks. 'The bridge is not supported by one stone or another,' Marco answers, 'but by the line of the arch that they form.' Kublai Khan remains silent, reflecting. Then he adds: 'Why do you speak to me of the stones? It is only the arch that matters to me.' Polo answers: 'Without stones there is no arch.'"—Italo Calvino, *Invisible Cities* (1978).

My friends, we are the stones and the arch is collapsing.

Why Him?

Every other person desires to lead the sheep as Martin Luther King, Banda Singh, or John F. Kennedy did. But only a handful of people are willing to make the financial and social sacrifices to learn what the true roots of the problems are. For this reason, positive change is hard to come by—the intention is there, but not the knowledge.

More importantly, too many are troubled when another person publicly voices their desire for change. In them arises hate and jealousy. "Why him?" And, "It should be me?" These are the two questions that provoke the animosity. These are the two questions that prevent unity.

The change this nation needs, in my lifetime, I will not see. Those who seek leadership lack the knowledge, and there is just too much hate and jealousy amid the people who require and desire a better existence.

To Sacrifice II

Positive change requires personal sacrifice. This, history suggests. There is no "ifs", "ands", or "buts". Check the books. The pleasures of the material world must be surrendered. Moreover, if a person does decide to sacrifice material things, a person will need to strengthen the mind so to endure the pain.

Soon after the decision to journey toward a better world is made, pain and suffering will begin their pursuit.

Perhaps, that's why so many compromise the greater good and evolve to adopt the attitude: *someone else will do it*. Besides, with so many material pleasures to be had, why invite pain and suffering into one's sphere of existence?

Until this attitude, which appears to be a hand-me-down value, given by the rulers to prevent the sheep from morphing into lions, is marginalized, no lasting positive change will manifest.

Life can be lived by dodging the responsibilities of a good citizen and a benevolent human, and the pain and suffering can be avoided. But more there is to the living than the living, and it does matter how a person lives and dies. Friends, the body is just a temporary vessel and within is the true "I" that continues. To this effect, there are multiple continuums, and those who sacrifice for the greater good invite the near-best celestial experience.

To sacrifice?

Enemies

A common enemy has united nations. A common enemy can unite the world. Do not look to another to see an enemy. Look to the ways of the world. Poverty - Hunger - Illiteracy. Consumption - Waste - Pollution. Jealousy - Hate - Divisions. Greed - War - Oppression.

CHAPTER 5

THE LAST HOPE

The last line of defence is openly assaulted and so many silently sit in the audience. This chapter will examine the manner in which the family unit is under attack.

The Family Divide

The family is the first and the last government. The family is the first and the last educational institution. The family is the first and the last temple. The family is the first and the last line of defence. But a family that's divided lives and dies powerless.

The culture of the consumer conditions the family to separate. By way of beliefs, when a child is the age of an adult, a family tends to divide.

This idea of leaving the nest is conditioned by the consumer culture because it stimulates the market—not to improve the existence of the human. You see, when an individual leaves the family, he or she will need the essentials of modern life such as cutlery, appliances, furniture, food, electricity, etc. This transition from the nest to the wilderness injects cash into the economy.

The more I think about the manufactured idea of separation, the more it feels as if there's a similarity between that notion and the idea of Christmas.

The notion of Christmas is no longer what it was and it was hijacked by corporate interests—it's no longer about love and Jesus but about purchasing and receiving.

During the Christmas season, most individuals feel there's only one-way to show their love for another, and that by purchasing a product or service and giving. An idea reinforced by conditioned expectations, and people believe love is predominantly shown through products and services. Because of this misguided notion, people expect products or services from people who care for them. Not only that, they judge the other's love by the products or services they give. It's more than evident that the notion of Christmas is no longer associated with the love demonstrated by Jesus, and the contemporary world has associated it with the act of giving and receiving products or services.

The idea of Christmas was hijacked by corporate interests so to inject cash into the economy, and the same is true of the family. It was also hijacked to syringe money.

The idea of Christmas was hijacked by associating it to the notion of giving and receiving products or services. The family was hijacked by associating ideas such as freedom, adulthood, individuality, and progress to separation. Most people believe that to attach these terms to their character, they must leave the family home. The idea of separation was so successfully associated and injected into the collective intelligence that most people believe it's natural to leave the nest at a given age—natural as the sun and the moon changing guard or winter coming after fall.

Most families have come to adopt the notion of separation but the value is inaccurate, artificial, and manipulative. The truth is that a person can still be an individual, with relative freedom, within a large family structure. More importantly, the want for individuality and freedom can be better satisfied through a family structure than by detaching from it.

I write "relative freedom" because absolute freedom is unobtainable. The freest one can be is to be least deterministic and that's a state of consciousness. In relation, before an individual can understand the notion of a least deterministic mind, or the idea of individuality, first, they must climb Maslow's pyramid. They must secure their physiological needs, their safety needs (security and protection), their social needs (belonging and love), and their esteem needs (recognition and status). Not surprisingly, it's easier to satisfy them within a family unit than detached from it.

An individual within a functional family structure has a greater potential to accumulate more resources than an individual who's left the nest. They can also exit the secular chase that pre-occupies most people much quicker, especially in today's costly world. This potential exists because of simple economics. Within a family unit, the household basics are not purchased by each individual, the mortgage payments are not on the shoulders of one or two but a few, and the household bills are divided. As such, an individual, within a functional family unit, has a greater potential to meet their physiological needs than an individual who stands separate.

An individual within a functional family also has a greater potential to secure their safety and social needs. Within a family unit, there's a sense of security and protection. A functional family provides a sense of safety due to the number of individuals in the unit, and from my experiences, the family rarely fails to protect a member when a member is in need of security and protection. And a person's social needs are easier to meet in a unit because no earthly entity can give unconditional love as a family can.

The same is true of a person's esteem needs and a functional family will recognize and appreciate the littlest and the greatest achievement, and they'll give an individual the encouragement and support required to achieve the small and the big.

The potential to realize the idea of freedom and individuality are greater within an extended family structure because it's easier for an individual to climb Maslow's mountain. As for the idea of adulthood, well, that's a state of consciousness.

Some parents understand the above and they try to restrain their children from leaving the nest. But the children don't understand. They push the propaganda of freedom, individuality, and adulthood to get away from their parents. If the family unit is functional, healthy, and allows a person to explore the ideas of individuality, adulthood, and freedom, then there's no need for a person to leave.

The culture of the consumer conditions the family to separate when the child is the age of an adult, and this belief is conditioned because it stimulates the market. Now, don't get me twisted, a person isn't less because he or she left the nest. There's absolutely nothing wrong with separating from a dysfunctional family. Sometimes, the only way to grow is to walk away from everything a person knows. But the built world is ruthless, and without guidance, sometimes, what grows is nothing more than a petal-less rose with a crooked stem.

The family is the first and the last government. The family is the first and the last educational institution. The family is the first and the last temple. The family is the first and the last line of defence. But a family that's divided lives and dies powerless.

The irrational cost to live forces people to create less children. The less children, the less potential for a family to generate wealth.

Single Parents

It can be inferred that the notion of divorce and the idea of a single parent also kindle the economy. Moreover, the ideas of divorce and a single parent are preyed upon by our popular culture. Take a look at the schedule of shows on the big screen and the television. Although they're not telling people to separate, they repeatedly showcase the phenomenon of a single parent as a common family structure, as a social norm, and this naturally desensitizes a person to the idea of divorce and raising a child alone.

Lust confused with love is also a powerful contributor to divorce, and just as powerful are the synthetic expectations of what a marriage should be. And not surprisingly, both are artificially inflated by the built world. As for the latter, when those unrealistic expectations are not repeatedly met by one of the partners in the marriage, the marriage is at risk. Unrealistic expectations such as a happy ending to almost every difficulty, the perfect social scenes, the feeling of love daily, and no financial worries are constantly popularized by popular media. These notions have brainwashed every other man and woman.

It can be inferred that the ideas of divorce and a single parent are manipulated so to stimulate the economy. To the detriment of the children. A child is at a disadvantage if raised by a single parent because they grow with half the resources, guidance, network, and protection. Even though they were silently promised the opposite during consummation. These children are divided and defeated before they even begin their quest. Tragic it is. But the market doesn't care so long as their god is satisfied. Greed motivates the market to do what it does and not the betterment of a person.

FX in Head

Unmatched divorce stats, unmatched single parents, unmatched degenerations, and unmatched causes. The contemporary popular culture has, for the time being, successfully broken the family unit.

And ugly are the consequences of a divided family. Everywhere the indicators be—beacons to unnatural tragedies. Nevertheless, they're concealed by special effects in head—illusions of nothing beyond death ahead are bred. It's similar to walking dead.

No place left for the little ones to grow to know. No one around to show, the idealist state in mind. Instead, their potential is denied. Instead, the little ones repeat and rewind.

....

The divorce experience devastates both man and woman. Yet, not enough is written about the man's experience and men seem to lose it all after a divorce, including their state of mind. Tens-of-millions of men are half dead inside because of the experience. Half dead men are easily defeated and pose little resistance.

Broken Connections

The family divide creates much destruction. Of this, I'd like to bring attention to a particular corruption. The family divide debases the transfer of higher knowledge.

The family divide corrupts the transfer of knowledge from generation to generation to generation. Although the built world doesn't truly instil ideas, beliefs, and wants able to uplift a person's value system, a parent eventually acquires some ideas, beliefs, and wants that uplift their value system. Unfortunately, because of the family divide, these ideas, beliefs, and wants of higher value aren't fully transferred from the parent to the child. Instead of building on the higher values housed by the parent, the child is rediscovering and relearning what their parent already knows.

A family unit, from generation to generation, can't truly progress, in the higher sense, so long as the family divide is a popular concept. Each generation is left to build from the foundation up instead of building floors above those built by their parents.

The families who survived the popular concept of the family divide will naturally reach higher with every passing generation. Of the masses, they have the best chance at rising above their status as servants.

Planted where the sun forgot to smile and the clouds forgot to speak, it probably wasn't that easy mimicking. So, if the strongest attribute of a rose is a crooked stem, please, do not love it any less.

"The first problem for all of us, men and women, is not to learn, but to unlearn." — Gloria Stienem

Raining Snake-Oil: The Last Line of Defence

The built world ignores a higher value system. Now, hope rests within the home. Now, the last line of defence is the family unit.

The family unit is able to instil a higher value system by structuring the home environment to communicate information that instils and reinforces the concept, and information that counterbalances and explains the information that might nurture the opposite.

It all sounds difficult. But how else to improve the human condition? Most other institutions able to influence an individual's value system have failed to instil higher values. In today's world, the only institution trustworthy enough to appropriately raise the children is the family institution.

To add to their hardships, a mortgaged life, a stack of bills, a nine-to-five, and household responsibilities take most of the family's time and energy. Little time and energy are left to raise the babies.

Be that as it may, there is no other choice if we wish to make the world a better place. One generation must take the road less traveled and sacrifice.

Sacrifice the artificially inflated worldly dreams and sacrifice to break the cognitive conditioning. Today's parents were raised by the same contaminated environments that raise today's children. First, the cycle must be broken. One generation must sacrifice the popular and create the ideal conditions so to breed the ideal person.

But a big problem this is. Far too many mind's were trained to point and blame and not evaluate the self and change. Positive criticism is a term foreign to their vocabulary. Try telling some adults that their cognitive content is missing something necessary and see what happens. They'll deny and justify almost everything. Stuck in a cycle. Stuck in a cycle and the little ones suffer.

The built world denies the right to experience through the highest state of awareness. Now, hope rests within the home. Now, the last line of defence is the family unit.

....

Children are more than mere objects. Wistfully, some parents can't understand this. Unenlightened themselves, they allow the cycle to continue and create an underdeveloped value system.

Shadow and Light

Sometimes a child is built to rebel and sometimes the parents are meant to learn. To those who understand and to those who didn't wave the white flag, thank you for exercising wisdom and patience, thank you for loving God's wild children, thank you for the countless sacrifices, and thank you for keeping the candle lit. The power over the shadow and the light belongs to those parents who understand.

"Those who educate children well are more to be honoured than parents, for these gave only life, those the art of living well." — Aristotle

Angels or Demons

Some people make inadequate parents and what I'm suggesting is that they lack the appropriate skills and knowledge. The stuff required to successfully raise the children, and denied are the children given. The children are denied a highly developed value system and the thoughts and actions pursuant.

Deeper still, affected are the communities they'll eventually lead, and affected are the children raised by tomorrow's cities. Denied are billions and billions.

Billions are denied because the values of the family have crumbled, and not surprisingly, the crumbling appears to positively correlate to the growth of neo-liberalism. It's as if this eco-political ideology built a factory and mass-produced inadequate parents. (To learn more about neo-liberalism, please read the book, *A Beautiful Destruction.*)

No child is a child forever and children become. Nevertheless, their potential is limited by information and inadequate parents can't possibly see the potential of children. Naively, they don't understand that children shine when amid diamonds. Childishly, they don't understand that children pass through and become, become as angels or demons.

It's a choice and not enough people are making it. Unaware, the art of living is uncommented. Unwittingly, most are offended by positive criticism.

Glossary

Amor patriae

Latin for: *Love for one's country.*

Audemus jura nostra defendere

Latin for: *To defend our rights we dare.*

Beautiful Cognitive Condition

The beautiful cognitive condition develops, houses, nurtures, and reinforces a value system constituted by such beliefs and wants as contentment, compassion, truth, unconditional love, humility, virtue, righteousness, empathy, self-actualization, a transitive conscious condition, rationality, emotional stability, a desire for knowledge, a spiritual life purpose (a life purpose before and beyond a secular purpose), a sense of oneness with humanity, and a **collective ego**.

Claustrum

The suspected part of the brain that, if stimulated, renders a person unconscious.

Collective ego

The ego represents the belief of the self. Although the substance of the ego is learned, the shell that houses that substance is innate. Not only this, the ego is the captain of both cognitive conditions and a person will grow to develop either a dominant collective ego or a dominant selfish ego. The characteristics of a collective ego are centered on the beautiful cognitive condition.

Collective Intelligence

The collective intelligence is constituted by the ideas, beliefs, wants, and knowledge most people have in common. The collective intelligence is typically transferred generation to generation, changing to reflect the changes that occur within the information popular culture communicates.

Cyrus the Great (580-529 B.C.)

> *"Cyrus was the first Achaemenian Emperor of Persia, who issued a decree on his aims and policies, later hailed as his charter of the rights of nations. Inscribed on a clay cylinder, this is known to be the first declaration of Human Rights, and is now kept at the British Museum. A replica of this is also at the United Nations in New York."*

[http://oznet.net/cyrus/cyframe.htm]

False Consciousness

The idea of a false consciousness was developed by Karl Marx and he suggested that most people are misled by the material and institutional processes of a capitalistic society. He also suggested that most people have a false understanding of capitalism and the nature of success, and they actually perpetuate the causes of their own unhappiness, suffering, and failure.

Gubernatio

Latin for: *pilotage; control; government.*

Lucius Quinctius Cincinnatus

A Roman citizen who was considered an example of Roman virtue. He gave back the office of dictator, and the absolute power accompanied by that post, after the crisis for which he was called to serve was resolved.

Middle-class peasant

A term used to represent the new type of socio-economic class that's emerged. It appears that the middle-class is losing and has lost the socio-economic conditions used to define them as middle-class. In addition, the traditional lower-class too sunk and neither the middle-class nor the lower-class fit into the traditional socio-economic models. For this reason, I consider the supposed middle-class as middle-class peasants.

Selfish Cognitive Condition

The dominant characteristics of a selfish cognitive condition are what trap a person's value system to the term "underdeveloped". The dominant characteristics of the selfish condition are beliefs that:

1)Suppress, weaken, contradict, or disguise the elements of the beautiful half.

2)Nurture only sensual fulfilment, a selfish existence, sensory satisfaction, individuality, and self interest.

3)Separate the self from humanity, communities, other people, The Absolute, the spirit, the Universe, and the planet.

4)Detail the individual with a higher value than humanity, other people, communities, death, The Absolute, the spirit, the Universe, and the planet.

5)Develop and nurture the **selfish ego** and the destructive elements that predominantly comprise the selfish ego.

Selfish ego

The selfish ego is centered on the beliefs mentioned above and the selfish ego is heavily constituted by the destructive elements. The four destructive elements within the mind are anger, lust, attachment, and greed. The destructive agents are so for several reasons. They intensify the alienation of the mind from the **beautiful cognitive condition** and the behaviour and thoughts it generates. They give rise for a person to hurt another. They are the most destructive attributes of the mind. They build and reinforce thoughts that strengthen the domination of a selfish cognitive condition. And they have a nasty habit of destroying the human condition from within.

1)Anger is an innate emotional unit of the mind. When the mind is influenced by the mental unit of anger, the mind predominantly turns onto the self. This state of perception naturally limits the information used by the mind's decision-making process.

2)Lust is an innate ability of the mind. It represents an intense and irrational want. Under the inductions of lust, the mind morphs into an island and is unable to construct thoughts outside the information that constitutes the irrational want.

3)Attachment is an innate ability of the mind. The term represents a mind unable to let go of a particular external or internal stimulation (memory, belief, or want). An attachment results in the narrowing of a person's awareness, and detachment from the stimulant usually causes the mind and body extreme pain and suffering.

4)Greed is a constructed want. It represents an irrational and unmastered appetite. The term is applicable to the senses as much as it is to an irrational appetite for material objects. As the others, greed alienates the mind from the power of the beautiful cognitive condition and all that follows.

Social contract

"Social Contract Theory, nearly as old as philosophy itself, is the view that persons' moral and/or political obligations are dependent upon a contract or agreement between them to form society."

[http://www.iep.utm.edu/s/soc-cont.htm]

The built world

The term symbolizes the neo-liberal/neo-conservative system of consumption, wealth extraction, resource extraction, production, and distribution. The term also encompasses the popular culture and the collective intelligence birthed by neo-liberalism/neo-conservatism. The term "built world" does not include the natural world.

The machine

The term "the machine" symbolizes the same as the term "the built world".

Thought Energy

"Thought Energy" is a term developed by the author to represent the time and space of the invisible place within an individual where a person thinks, feels, sees, etc. Thought Energy is the truest "I".

Veil of Ignorance

"John Rawls proposed a method, which he called the veil of ignorance, for determining which social customs were just and which were unjust. The veil of ignorance criterion is as follows: a rule is just if everyone would agree to it given that they were made ignorant of their position in society. That is, the just society would be chosen by people who had set aside considerations of their own gender, wealth, race, parentage,

etc. Ideally this rule eliminates personal bias from the choice and thus guarantees the fairness of rules."
[http://onphilosophy.wordpress.com/2006/05/05/beyond-the-veil-of-ignorance/]

Warrior-Poet

The one with a humorous and sweet tongue, a lion's heart, a worldly outlook, and a link to God.

The one with a philosopher king's mentality, a saint's humility, the compassion and honour of Saladin, and who serves humanity like Jassa Singh.

The one who lives to die for the greater good, journeys within the material world but is detached from, exists in the absolute realm, and cherishes truth, knowledge, virtue, and freedom.

The one whose strength is gained from Naam, whose mind's eye is with God, whose spirit is ironclad, and whose essence is the weak person's to command.

The one mesomorphic as the male offspring of Cronus—the Titan, quick as those who sprint the 100 meter in under 10 seconds, enduring as a marathon champion, and athletic as a multi-event gold medal Olympian.

This, my friends, is a Warrior-Poet.

Western caste system
From the top to the bottom:
1) Filthy rich and educated
2) Filthy rich and uneducated

3) Rich and educated

4) Rich and uneducated

5) Middle-class peasants and educated

6) Middle-class peasants and uneducated

7) Poor and educated

8) Poor and uneducated

Each caste has different potentials and each caste has different options available to them. Moreover, all people are born into a caste, and the higher up the ladder one is born, the higher the degree of freedom one has the potential to secure.

"It is not the critic who counts; not the man who points out how the strong man stumbles, or where the doer of deeds could have done them better. The credit belongs to the man who is actually in the arena, whose face is marred by dust and sweat and blood; who strives valiantly; who errs, who comes short again and again, because there is no effort without error and shortcoming; but who does actually strive to do the deeds; who knows great enthusiasms, the great devotions; who spends himself in a worthy cause; who at the best knows in the end the triumph of high achievement, and who at the worst, if he fails, at least fails while daring greatly, so that his place shall never be with those cold and timid souls who neither know victory nor defeat." — Excerpt from the speech, Citizen in a Republic: the man in the arena, given by Theodore Roosevelt.

Without a sword or a Tommy-gun, in the arena I am. My weapon of choice is the pen, and marred by dust, sweat, and ink, weak-kneed I stand—gazing at the sun to increase my strength.

I wonder—will a day come, before I fall, that witnesses a benevolent king or queen riding through the theatre gates? One able to smash the darkness. One worthy of the divine right. One akin to the Great Gobind Singh. Such a personality is required if we, the sheep, wish to improve humanity.

Made in the USA
Columbia, SC
13 June 2020